Build It!

DIY Projects for Farmers, Smallholders
and Gardeners

D0063216

By Joe Jacobs

ISBN 978 1 90487 132 3
A catalogue record for this book is available from
the British Library.

Published by
The Good Life Press Ltd.
PO Box 536
Preston
PR2 9ZY

www.goodlifepress.co.uk

Set by The Good Life Press Ltd.
Illustrations and photographs © by Joe Jacobs
Printed and bound in Great Britain
by Cromwell Press

Contents

Introduction

If a book on smallholding projects were to have an aim, it would have to be the successful completion of the projects listed therein. The trouble is, many prospective DIY readers possess differing levels of skill; you may feel that your personal handiwork might fall into the general categories of good, bad or indifferent. Doing it one's self is supposed to be fun rather than infuriating but things in life do not always quite turn out as expected. Several of this author's past projects have ended up as unmitigated failures. Don't despair if things don't work out quite right the first time; simply pick up the bits and start again.

Please do not think of this book as a rigid set of blueprints but as a guide and an inspiration for some daft ideas of your own. After you've cursed for the umpteenth time and have two cut hands and a blackened nail, simply go out and buy one of whatever it was you were trying to build.

Visiting other people's smallholdings is a great way of

changing one's perspective on how something can be done. That said, it does not necessarily follow that foreign ideas will transplant successfully into your own situation. There are those holdings with perfectly trimmed borders and plenty of shiny new equipment but for most of us, fifty percent of the farming battle is against mud, wind, rain and broken farm machinery. A great deal of time can be wasted trying to mend farm equipment and it sometimes really does pay to just go out and buy a new one. Economy of effort is an over-riding principle in both the maintenance and construction of items on the smallholding. Is the time spent on a project worth the end result?

Of course in farming if we were to price our time it would by and large be a joke anyway; I am persuaded that certain things are worth doing simply because we enjoy them.

Lastly, neither the author or publishers take any responsibility for accidents or disasters resulting from attempts to replicate the projects illustrated in this book.

DIY, the only thing potentially worse than working with children or animals.

Joe Jacobs
North Yorkshire
2008

Acknowledgements

I would like to thank the following people who, through their help or advice, have inadvertently contributed to the fabrication of this book. My good lady Dr. F. Jacobs and little TZJ, V. Jacobs, B. Dicker, D. Sanderson, P. Scrope, P. Crawford, K. Hornby, all my animals, Mostyn Dog and, last but not at all least, the publishers.

Great workshop, unfortunately all the space is used.

Chapter One
The Workshop and Tools

There are items that I would not go out and buy even if I won the lottery because I can't help but think of them as an extraordinary waste of money. In these rural parts, wages are little above minimum and high paid work is difficult to come by. Therefore there is little point in lining someone else's pocket with money spent on goods that have, in effect, a labour charge of £100 a day or more added to their material cost. What did the item cost to make? If one cannot earn that perceived labour charge of say £100 in the time it would take to manufacture the item, then it is undoubtedly worth a DIY attempt. Often materials for wooden projects are relatively cheap and in many a case can even be reclaimed or acquired for nothing but it's not always cost alone that governs a project's viability. Other factors to consider include:

- Functionality - something may not be commercially available like that which you need or have in mind.

- Fun – you are doing it because you fancy making the project for its own sake.

- Availability - it may be possible that what you need is not available locally.

- Time – there are rare occasions when it's quicker to build something than go shopping or wait for one to be posted.

The Notion of a Workshop and Suitable Tools

Having spent a great deal of time and money renovating a barn which could be used as a workshop, it is now so stuffed full of tools, junk and rubbish that it is impossible to reach the very useful pillar drill in the corner. The notion is there but my workshop, to all intents and purposes, is not.

Many large woodworking projects can be undertaken outside on a fair weather day. Let's face it, unless you have a nice cosy heated workshop, it can be pretty miserable working inside in the cold as opposed to outside in the cold. Provided, of course, that it is not raining or overly windy, I much prefer to strew my tools around a large open area and construct projects in the fresh air. In singing the praises of the great outdoors, we must also briefly consider the functionality of a workshop if one were to be available. Entire books have been devoted to the setting up of workshops. This is not one of them. Here are a few simple tips; the following assets, in some guise or other, are desirable for project work:

Workbench – this is a must and provides a level surface on which items may be screwed, glued and assembled. If a decent bench is unavailable, a portable fold out 20 quid bench is better than nothing.

Vice – You may have plenty of these but only a good solid metal one will do for DIY projects. To utilise a vice to its full capacity, it should be bolted to a bench. If you are privileged enough to own a long work bench, a vice at each end can be a great boon for holding objects that need cutting or drilling.

Storage

There are two fields of thought on this. Storage is very useful if you know where to look for the stored items. The other field of thought is to have a more organised mind and a less organised workshop. I vaguely consider time spent scrupulously tidying tools away to be time wasted, although I rarely loose tools. Shelving is certainly useful as it enables one to clear away the vast quantities of junk that may accumulate underfoot. So you can stuff your cupboards, I'll always opt for more shelves please. Shelves do also have the added bonus of displaying what is on them.

Tools

Don't despair if your tool collection is little more than a pair of rusty scissors and a twisted screwdriver. The price of tools has plummeted and some of the cheapest really aren't bad at all. A selection of hand tools is a must. What follows is not an exhaustive list but a guide for the uninitiated of the bare essentials required for simple woodworking and other projects.

In the last five years the cost of power tools has decreased dramatically and whilst the quality of various brands is debatable, these machines can cut huge swathes of time out of DIY projects. You can carry out projects without power tools but it takes a hell of a lot longer and a requires a lot more physical effort.

Hand Tools

A basic tool kit should comprise of at least the following:

Hammer – There are various designs but a claw hammer is about the most useful for agricultural wood work, the claw enabling you to remove all those bent and mis-hit nails from your projects.

Screwdrivers – Cheap screwdrivers don't last very long as the heads are not usually hard enough. A selection of flat and cross heads with hardened tips is useful. Alternatively, cordless drill / drivers are handy but they do require frequent recharging.

Wood Saws – A couple of useful wood saws (not old blunt ones) are essential for project work. A tenon saw is the short type with a reinforcing strip along its top edge and is very useful for short straight cuts where accuracy is required. A general purpose crosscut saw (the bendy 2-3ft long type of saw) can be used for anything from cutting plywood to sawing through heavy timbers.

Hack Saw - Necessary for cutting anything made of metal. The blade is tensioned by a wing nut which tightens. The saw will not cut correctly unless the blade is properly adjusted. A junior hacksaw is also a useful addition to a toolkit and can be used to cut in situ metalwork where there may not be room enough to wield a full size saw.

Spanners - A selection of spanners typically covering 6,8,10 and 12mm are useful for projects where bolts are a better design option than screws. A couple of adjustable spanners may suffice equally well.

Pliers - There are many designs of pliers and they may be used for anything from loosening rounded nuts and bolts to retrieving items dropped into inaccessible places. Buy a standard set of pliers, a set of needle nose pliers and a pair of wire cutters.

Measurement - A steel rule, a tape measure and a set square for marking 90 and 45 degree cuts should be in your tool kit. There are odd occasions when a protractor might also come in handy. Curves and arcs are best marked using a pencil and a length of string pinned at one end.

Sandpaper - Can be used to smooth off rough wooden edges. If things look really bad and power tools are not available then a surform is probably what you need. Sandpaper comes in a myriad of grades. It's probably best to buy a pack of mixed sheets, then you'll hopefully have all eventualities covered.

Knife - In addition to the obligatory farmer's pocket knife, a sharper type of craft knife is useful. Most jobs require the use of a knife, even if it's only to open the awkward packaging of a box of screws. The thin, snap off blade variety never seem to last very long. The Stanley knife design is a better option and is more controllable in the hand.

There are plenty of other tools that are desirable for DIY projects, but the only one that I personally would not be without is my Yankee screwdriver. Manufactured by Stanley tools, the Yankee is a long, ratcheted, changeable bit screwdriver. When you push down on the handle, the tool bit rotates.

Yankee screwdrivers require some physical effort to operate, however, they are far quicker to use than putting in screws using a conventional driver and, unlike cordless battery models, they do not require frequent recharging.

Power Tools

There are some very good power tools on the market, there are also some very bad ones. Hopefully this short guide will help you to make a selection that doesn't end up wasting your hard earned moolah. There are some very big names in power tools with corresponding big prices, although the quality is usually excellent. Many of the cheap Chinese import power tools come with spare drive belts and motor brushes which are a joke because the product will have ground itself into oblivion long before the spare parts are needed.

The answer lies herein. Big companies like B&Q and Homebase cannot afford to have their good names sullied by trash products and therefore spend a great deal of time sourcing decent budget power tools. All the power tools I have purchased from B&Q's basic range have served me faultlessly on a house building project for several years, but most of the other cheap imports I have used have died very quickly indeed. In some cases (especially 9 inch angle grinders for some reason) tools have packed up within just a few hours of being put to work. If it looks very cheap and plasticky, then don't buy it.

Drills - These days one can buy an electric drill to suit almost any occasion, although in reality one is probably all you'll ever need. I've fallen out of love with cordless battery products, not because they don't work or lack oomph, but because I too often neglect or forget to charge them. Buy a variable speed mains drill and it shouldn't see you far wrong. If it is your intention to do metalwork on a regular basis then you may want to invest in a suitable pillar drill or drill press. As these upright drills are by no means cheap to come by, it may be wise to look out for a secondhand one, either on the internet or at local auctions.

Electric Saws - There are a plethora of designs of electric saws and all are useful but some more so than others. A jigsaw (or pendulum saw) with a selection of blades can be used for most project woodcutting applications although they do not have the greatest cutting speed in the world. Circular saws are not ideal for accurate cutting work although they come into their own for rip sawing and cutting straight lines in large sheets of plywood. It is now possible to buy a small portable bench saw for as little as thirty pounds and to my mind these are a better investment than a circular saw. The two are essentially the same anyway except that the bench saw is upturned and mounted into a metal bench. Instead of having what is in effect a circular saw mounted in a bench, it is also possible to have one mounted over an adjustable table. These are known as mitre saws and are available as either fixed or sliding. Sliding cross cut saws are extremely useful for cutting timber to a precise angle eg. 45 degrees, 30 degrees etc. The limitation of a crosscut saw is that it is only possible to cut timber up to about 300mm wide with a sliding saw and perhaps as little as 80mm wide with a fixed mitre saw. To anybody with no power tools at all I would suggest that a jigsaw is a very useful piece of kit and that a bench saw would make a good investment but a circular saw would make a cheaper alternative to the bench variety.

There are inevitably rough edges that ought to be removed from any wooden items and sandpaper, files and planes are all great, but if it's a large job then electric planes and sanders really come into their own.

Sheet sanders are cheap and are an effective way of achieving a smooth finish on wood that is not overly rough in nature. If the timber is particularly roughly sawn, then a plane may be more suitable for any smoothing work. For jobs where the removal of a significant amount of material is required then a belt sander could be what is required. These devices need particular vigilance when in use as they will literally eat through your job in no time at all.

There are plenty of other power tools not listed here that may enhance any job, however, in summary, 2 saws and a drill should suffice for the following chapters.

Working Safely

Having rambled on about a few of the tools necessary to practise DIY, it might now be worth dwelling on a few of the pitfalls awaiting the unwary. As someone who is relatively safety conscious, I have still had 3 avoidable minor accidents in the past year. These mishaps have resulted from practical projects and one of these could have required a hospital visit, were it not for the doctoring skills of my good lady.

Eye protection is paramount for most practical jobs; the discomfort of sawdust in the eye is nothing compared to what could happen if a random wood fragment thrown out of a power saw hit home. We only have one pair of eyes, so protect them. The protection of hearing is often forgotten and whilst you may not consider a noise to be particularly loud, prolonged exposure to it may damage your hearing. Earplugs are cheap so use them. If working in a confined area, wood dust can become a major irritant to the respiratory system. Unfortunately power tools are to blame for very fine saw dust so there are times when a simpleand cheap face mask may be an advantage. This same airborne saw dust is also a major fire hazard. Whilst woodwork is difficult if wearing gloves, there are projects listed herein that will require them. Rigger gloves and nitrile dipped builders gloves cost about 99p a pair and they don't half save your hands from some painful wear and tear.

Perhaps the biggest risk when working with power tools and extension leads is that of electrocution. Very few people know the state of the earthing system in their house and whether it really represents a more attractive pathway to electricity than the hapless tool holder. If your electricity system is not fitted with an RCD (residual current device) then you would be well advised to get one as it would offer a degree of protection in the event of chopping through your wires. An RCD will cut the supply in the event of it detecting current leakage to earth. RCD's are now available as in-line units and may even be incorporated in some extension reels. Fire could also be a potential hazard when working indoors. There is little to say on this subject apart from be aware of the potential hazard of overloading electrical circuits with lots of devices, all plugged in simultaneously. Small, low cost fire extinguishers are available for about £10 and represent, along with a first aid kit, a very worthy workplace investment.

As has oft been stated, one should never work with children or animals. Never a truer word was spoken when it comes to DIY tasks. Know the whereabouts of any kids and dogs and keep them well out of the way. The last piece of advice I shall give actually results from a very painful personal lesson. Don't leave any heavy objects either on dodgy workbenches or on a table edge because they tend to fall off, and it will usually be on you.

Build It!

Materials

The general idea of DIY is that it keeps the cost of work down although this doesn't always ring true. After several years of working on a smallholding/renovation project I'd consider myself a veritable expert on saving money. The following paragraphs are largely orientated towards purchasing timber as this is often where the greatest savings can be made.

Where to Buy Timber

The problem with buying timber is that the outlets that sell it will not offer you, the consumer, the best prices the first time that you walk through the door. Whilst B&Q and the large DIY stores do sell wood, they don't generally offer very competitive prices. If it's wood you're after then go to a timber yard and if there isn't a bespoke one in your locality then try a builders' merchant. Be aware of what other retailers are charging for the products that you are purchasing and don't be afraid to ask for a discount. Some of the larger chains of builders merchant have far too many prices for one product; the price you are offered depends very much on who you, the customer, are. Tell them what the item costs elsewhere and dig your heels in!

Roughly sawn timber can also be purchased at very economical rates from a sawmill if there is one in your neighbourhood. Usually it will be unseasoned and it may be the by-product of another process such as cutting fence posts. Small mills may also cut to your own specifications with a little advance notice. Sawmills are a great place to buy inexpensive timber but you really do need a range of power tools to continue the cutting and finishing of the wood. Timber can be recycled, so don't go throwing away or burning any sound material that might be incorporated into some future design. In the last few years there has been a great proliferation of salvage reclamation yards. These places are often interesting to say the least and are not all expensive. Timber can often be found in great quantities in these yards. As you will see, I built a very comfortable double bed for a meagre £7 worth of reclaimed wood.

Regional and local weekly papers are a great source of information regarding any local auctions and sales. The amount of quality timber I have seen sold at auction, especially at farm dispersal sales, for a fraction of its true worth beggars belief. As I write, it is not one month since I paid £12 for timber in an auction that would have cost in excess of £150 from a timber yard.

What to Buy

It's fairly obvious that what to buy is largely dependent on the project in hand. What may not be so evident, however, is the vast range of grades of timber available to the consumer, and naturally these are marked by substantial price differences. Plywood generally comes in three different grades and a variety of thicknesses. There's a basic grade of shuttering or exterior plywood which usually has a fairly knotty finish and, to all intents and purposes, looks pretty yellowy. The better grades of exterior ply will have a decent finish on one side. The best quality stuff is what most people refer to as marine ply. Interior plywood has been laminated with a different type of glue and is not suitable for long term outdoor usage. The difference between the grades is not only the quality of the glue but also the number and quality of the laminations within the ply. If one were to leave three untreated pieces of respective ply grades outside, it is highly likely that de-lamination caused by water ingress would have started to affect the budget exterior grade long before the better grades.

In essence, the life of plywood is directly proportional to the amount of treatment it gets; if the exposed edges are sealed with a quality treatment, then the product will last for many years. Other heavier timbers are likewise available in varying grades. Generally speaking, timber is either sold as planed or otherwise. Planed softwood timber may be categorised according to grain quality, knots etc. The cheapest grades may simply be referred to as something like budget or contract. Unplaned timber may be labeled according to its intended purpose eg. laths, ridge board, carcassing etc. Timber that was primarily designed for roofing may also be available as treated or untreated. For structural woodwork it is possible to buy heavy timbers that have been inspected and graded as to their suitability for purpose.

Sourcing Parts for Projects

I was once castigated in a magazine for not supporting local businesses in my enthusiasm for the next two topics, eBay and Screwfix. The fact of the matter is that small local businesses certainly have their place in the world but if it comes to large orders, then you really cannot beat the larger hardware retailers. At this point if you are choking with rage, please forgive me; it's only an opinion but it is a valid one.

I was aware of Screwfix, the mail order company, some years ago, but it was a while before I first ordered from them. This delay was a costly mistake. Selling everything from screws to power tools, plumbing to sheds, this trade hardware company is often hard to beat on price. That said, I'm not convinced that their power tool prices are overly competitive but the company must be doing well because they've now opened a network of walk-in trade counters around the country. The local retailer does have an advantage here because, unless you order £45 worth of gear from Screwfix, you have to pay a postal charge which is, I suppose, fair enough. Their delivery service is, however, pretty good so you shouldn't be kept waiting very long for your goods. Orders can be made over the phone or online at www.screwfix.com.

It would be impossible to write about the procurement of cheap goods without considering eBay. As someone very experienced in its subtle nuances, I have to confess to losing faith a little after losing £200 to a rogue trader in 2006. However, as a source of buying low cost products it really does excel. It's very easy to check the prices of things against eBay and you might be surprised to find that it probably would be the cheapest place to buy a set of plastic wheels for your mobile hayrack.

Design

When designing objects for use on the smallholding folks....... What's that you say, designing? All too often projects are hastily screwed together with little thought being given other than to the end of the job. This construction method is a complete waste of time and can be, at the very least, dangerous for the end user be it a chicken or a goat. Even if you do not sit down with a pencil and paper, which I incidentally frequently do, there are a few criteria which ought to be considered before starting a DIY project.

A few years ago I designed a chicken house that could be flat packed. Here's a rough outline of the thought process behind that design. Consider the following design process and think of ways you could apply it to your own projects.

Firstly, the proposed chicken ark was to be for sale and was therefore to be posted within the confines of the Royal Mail parcel service. This dictated its maximum size and weight.

The item was to have a set price and would therefore not want to exceed a given material cost. The design was therefore to be cut from a single sheet of exterior grade 9mm plywood and a few regularly available offcuts.

Build It!

4mm ply would probably not have been strong enough. Bear in mind that chicken muck rots wood so either 9 or 12mm ply would be more appropriate and in order to hold the structure togethe securely, the ends and partitions were designed to be made from 18mm plywood.

Although it would be possible to make a chicken house from 4mm ply, it would probably not last very long. Design your creations so that they last for as long as possible before destruction or renovation.

The function in this instance was to build an economic house for up to 4 birds with an integral nesting area. The finished design was fit for the function for which it was intended. If you are building a pig house, or indeed a stable, the end product must be fit for purpose. Durability and strength are both key issues of the function which must, in turn, endanger neither persons nor livestock.

Form is also a consideration, by which we simply mean does it look nice? Sure, I can build a dog kennel out of pallet wood but constructing one to be proud of could be a different matter. I find a coat of paint always helps.

I'm not sure if the word 'workability' is exactly suited, but what you are building does need to be designed with ease of manufacture in mind. Project woodwork should be designed so that the least number of components are necessary without compromising strength. Consider the fixings you might need. Have you already got them and are they strong enough?

Some of these criteria might not apply to every task you undertake but they can form the basis of some sort of coherent design strategy for your future projects. Some of the greatest engineering feats in this country were done by a certain Mr I. K. Brunel. It would be fair to say that over the last 150 years or so none of his works have fallen down because they are immensely strong and were built to last. There is a certain amount of common sense in eyeballing something and knowing it is up to the job, and certainly Brunel's work tended to be on the safe side of heavy engineering. When building a structure, if in doubt use the heavier timber. That way, even if the project is a failure, in a year's time it might burn better.

Fastenings

Nails have their place in fabrication but past experience has shown that they only get forced or fall apart. Substantial screws are undoubtedly the best form of general fastening. For projects that might be directly in contact with large animals, use coach bolts, washers and nuts. A 6mm bolt is appropriate for sheep and small pigs. If I were building anything aimed at cattle or horses, I would use 8 or 10mm bolts or, alternatively, a threaded bar cut to the required length.

A Note on Units of Measurement

Everybody seems to know what a length of 4 x 2 inch timber looks like. If I were to offer a piece of 101.6 x 50.8 nobody would know what the hell I was on about. Both units of measurement have their place. There are simply 2.54cm in one imperial inch and both standards of measurement are used in this book, I'm not going to quote something as 81.3cm when 3ft would have sufficed or 15.75 inches when a simple 40cm would have done. Many things in British life were and still are built to an imperial standard and ultimately, for the purposes of DIY and engineering, one needs to be able to adopt both systems.

And so, armed only with a toolbox, without further ado........
DIY projects for farmers, smallholders and gardeners.

Build It!

Trailer top in use. The ramp is fastened up with penny washers and 2 wing nuts.

Chapter Two
Projects for the Barn and Field

Simple Livestock Trailer Top

This idea came about due to the need for a road going trailer that would be able to carry two or three sheep. Small livestock trailers are not easy to come by and the balloon tyred quad trailers are not road legal for towing behind a car. I considered the possibility of making a simple top for a conventional trailer and quickly got on the case. The beauty of this idea is that you do not lose your trailer for other uses and can simply remove the top when it is not required. You may already have a suitable trailer to which you can adapt this design but if you haven't, don't go and buy the first secondhand one you see. You must always check the condition underneath a trailer, the suspension, the tyres and the condition of the wheel bearings. Determine the state of the bearings by giving the tyres a pull and a push with both

Build It!

hands; this should show whether there is any slack or play.

For a very reasonable £60 I bought a 4ft x 3ft trailer with an almost perfect drop down tailgate locally. This size of trailer, or anything similar that you may have, could easily have a top made for it that would enable it to safely transport sheep, goats or small pigs. Structurally, a trailer intended for moving animals needs to be of a sturdy build. From the outset I chose to use plenty of 6mm coach bolts to ensure that the project could not be kicked apart whilst in use. Timber used in this instance was actually 3 x 1.25″ (approx. 76 x 32mm) fencing rails from the local sawmill. The uprights in the corners of the trailer are all 2 x 1.5″ (50 x 38mm). A roof can be made from 12mm ply if you have plenty to hand and the 3 x 1.25″ rails could all be replaced by sheet ply, although the finished article will not last as long.

How to........

Cut six lengths of 2 x 1.5″ (50 x 38mm) or equivalent to a height that will allow your largest sheep to stand upright ie. between 0.8 and 1m. In this instance it was 0.82m. These are the main corner and intermediary posts to which the top and sides of the structure will be bolted. As well as uprights in each corner of the structure, you will need the same every 2ft (0.6m) along the sides. If your donor trailer is 4ft wide, I would suggest a post in the middle of the leading end as well.

Ten lengths of 4 x 1″ (100x25mm) should be cut to the length of your donor trailer and five pieces cut to the width of the trailer. In this example 10 lengths of 4ft and 5 lengths of 3ft were cut.

The top is made so that it is, in effect, a stand alone structure. The six 'legs' will stand in the corners and along the sides of the existing trailer and they will be secured to it by bolts.

Start by constructing one side of the trailer. The uprights should be able to stand in their respective corners. The planks will, in all probability, overlap the uprights at each end by between 1 and 2 inches.

Plank No.

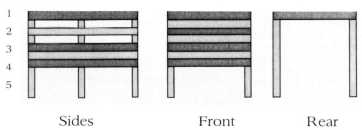

| Sides | Front | Rear |

The planks numbered 1, 3 and 5 (darker grey) are secured to their uprights using coach bolts, washers and nuts; nylon locking nuts are best. For good measure, add a wood screw above and below each bolt. The remaining planks (lighter grey) are secured using suitable length wood screws, two at each joint. 45 mm screws were used for this job.

Livestock trailer top. Note the use of coach bolts and strong timbers.

It shouldn't take too much explanation to see how the rest of the structure fits together as they say that "a picture paints a thousand words." Note the two triangular top pieces at the ends. These are screwed down into the timber below using 3″ screws. The rigid structure should stand comfortably in the trailer and the bottom planks should rest neatly on the trailer sides. The trailer does, of course, need a top to stop its precious cargo jumping out again so a length of the same

Build It!

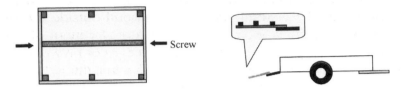

material used for the uprights should be screwed in place to form a central roof beam. (See above diagram)

A roof can be made from two separate pieces of plywood which, in this example, are 48cm wide by 120cm (4ft) long. There is obviously sufficient body of wood to screw the roof to. Plenty of fixings should be used as strength really is the key issue and the screws should be positioned approximately 10cm apart all the way around each roof sheet. A set of four long bolts are needed in order to fix the top to your trailer. I can't recommend lengths as these will vary depending on the trailer you use. The trailer will need four holes drilling in it, corresponding to the positions of the corner legs. The bolts are situated approximately 6″ up from the trailer floor. The fixings run through each leg from the inside of the trailer, through the trailer side where they are washered and bolted on the outside. The top may be removed by simply unscrewing the nuts and tapping the bolts back out.

I was lucky enough to start this project with a trailer that had a suitable tailgate which closed high enough to act as a back door for the trailer and provide a ramp. You may need to extend the back door of your trailer with a piece of 22mm ply bolted with four bolts to the inside of your existing drop down tailgate. Any ramp that you decide to make should have some lengths of batten screwed to it to give your sheep something to climb up on. If you extend your ramp to form a back door, be aware it needs a method of securing it in transit. In our design we used bolts and wing nuts although off the shelf door bolts could easily be made to keep the ramp shut.

The trailer was treated with creocote (one of the modern equivalents of creosote) and has sat around outside for 18 months with no ill effects, save the roof. I cannot stress enough the importance of treating the edges of plywood to stop it de-laminating. Armed with a suitable lighting board, the trailer is road legal and can fit in two adult sheep, and is thus a great asset to any smallholding.

Pallets are fit for a variety of uses.

Gates and Hurdles

When it comes to working with sheep and pigs, you simply cannot ever have enough gates and hurdles. Combined with plenty of 'band' (baling twine for those not in the know) and a sharp pocket knife, gates and hurdles can be used for making temporary pens and crushes for sorting and treating livestock. Gates and hurdles come in practically any size, but typical off the shelf metal sizes are 6, 8, 10, 12, 15 and 16ft, with gates usually made of either wood or steel. Metal gates are great but sheep hurdles alone cost over £20 each and 10ft gates are at least £50 each. I would like to have all metal galvanised gates but the cost is too prohibitive.

Build It!

Hurdle from a wooden pallet. Planks removed from one side to reinforce the other.

A cheap but slightly heavy option is to use pallets for making small enclosures. The type of pallet that is closely boarded on both sides is very useful for making temporary chicken runs for growers, with just 3 or 4 pallets and a bit of netting for the top so that the birds cannot escape. The heavy pallets are also very good for using as gates in pig sties. Pallets of the more flimsy variety (ie. the boarding is not so close together) can very easily be turned into lightweight hurdles. Using a claw hammer or a crow bar, carefully prise off the 4 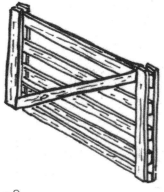 or so boards from one side of the pallet. Turn the pallet over and re-attach them, filling in the gaps between the other planks. The longer the pallet, the more useful the finished article.

How to make a small gate

From the main pictures it may

seem obvious enough. The real strength in the gates lies in the diagonal cross bracings. These stop the gates from sagging and help to spread the load. It's worth ensuring that, when making a gate, you spend a little time to ensure that the saw cuts on the Z butt together nicely. The top illustration is a good design for any longer gates and the illustration at the botom is in common usage amongst many makers of wooden sheep hurdles. The central illustration is a typical picket fencing type of gate and is fairly strong, looks nice and is relatively easy to make. Timber selection is important if you want

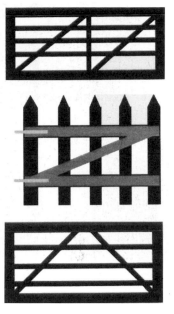

a gate to last. A gate that is too heavy is a no go but neither is a gate that is too flimsy. A small picket gate, as illustrated, works nicely with palisades of about 100 x 20mm. Bracing, however, needs to be a little heavier and in this example it was 50 x 25mm (2 x 1") and made using a roofng batten. A large gate really needs substantial timber, say something like 3 x 1.5". To avoid morticing the uprights at either end of the gates (cutting holes for the gate bars to fit into), use a sandwich construction where the horizontal bars are held by a separate piece of timber on each side of the gate. (See diagram on previous page)

Stone Planter / Trough

Stone troughs are worth a bomb round where we live. I dug three small ones out of the ruins of a barn wall. The best use for them is not pansies or begonias but what they were originally intended for; animals. My pigs have not turned over or broken my stone troughs and they are used for both watering and feeding. As we have a surfeit of sandstone

Build It!

in these parts I have tried to manufacture my own troughs and, with patience and the right tools, it is possible, but the hardest part is undeniably finding the right piece of stone. Granite and sandstone can be worked with relative ease, but I'm not sure about other stone types. Limestone is porous and is not really suited to this work. Having found a suitable stone you will need gloves, goggles, a lump hammer, a selection of chisels and a 4.5″ angle grinder with cutting discs. An SDS drill with chisel can also be useful. Stone is far easier to work if wet, but it needs to be saturated, not just rained upon. Wet stone has either been sitting somewhere damp or has been buried for a long time.

Start by squaring up your block. Use the angle grinder to make large cuts where necessary and use the hammer to knock the excess piece off. When you have a relatively square block to work from, start by marking out the top of the trough. Make the four long cuts that delineate the sides with the grinder, making sure you leave a good thickness around the

Not antique stone troughs but home made reproductions from suitable stones. We have the benefit of help from power tools over the hammers and chisels used by masons of old.

edges Carefully divide this square up with more cuts (rather like a chessboard). Using a hammer and chisel, knock out the chessboard squares one at a time. Keep repeating this grinder / chisel exercise until your trough reaches sufficient depth. Smooth grinder marks can be textured and removed with careful use of a bolster chisel. With care a trough can be finished to a good standard and, if left to weather outside for a winter, it may even look original.

Concrete Troughs

Concrete troughs can easily be cast at home and are an inexpensive way of creating feed or water containers. Start by constructing a box out of 18mm plywood to the size you want your finished trough to be. Aim to cast the walls of the trough about 65mm (2.5″) thick so that the trough maintains a degree of strength. Construct a second box that will fit inside the first one leaving a 2.5″ gap all the way around. A good cheat is to use a cheap plastic storage container as the inner mould which will hold about 40 litres of water. Construct the outer wooden box to be 130mm longer, 130mm wider and 65mm deeper.

To cast a trough make up a fairly strong concrete mix tending to the wet side as follows:

3 shovels of sharp sand, one shovel of pea gravel, one shovel of cement. Ensure the mix is thorough with no dry material left in it. Put an even 2.5 inches of concrete in the bottom of the large wooden mould and use a piece of wood to agitate (up and down motion) the concrete to help rid it of air pockets. Level the wet base and place the inner plastic container on top of it. What now remains is the job of carefully filling up the sides whilst trying to keep the plastic container central. Work your way around the container a little at a time and try to ensure that the concrete is well tamped down.

Build It!

Leave it to set completely. Concrete might seem sturdy after 24 hours in dry weather but it certainly hasn't really achieved its full structural strength. Removing the inner plastic after 48 hours will aid drying but do err on the side of caution and leave the trough for at least a few days more before moving it anywhere. If, after removing the mould, you find large air pockets or pock marks, you can always point these with a small mix of cement.

Improvised Feed Bins

It is said that if you keep chickens or pigs, you keep rats. It is certain that rats are very intelligent animals and are soon able to link the regular feeding of other animals with their own parasitic ways. Regular poisoning of rats helps to control them but, in order to do this effectively, we must first remove the offending food sources. Feeding poultry close to dusk leaves margin for error as they do not always eat it all. The other major rat objective is to find your feed store. I recently had one ton of bagged pig food stored in a barn and lost between five and ten percent of it to rats. I know this because all the wasted bags were at the bottom. By any rate that is a lot of food and it certainly isn't cheap. I now have steel feed hoppers.

Plastic wheelie bins make excellent bulk feed containers with the added benefit that they can be moved about. The plastic is of a high grade and I haven't seen any attempts to gnaw through it. One of the best feed bins I have for loose grain is a 45 gallon oil drum that has had the top cut out. I paid £5 for this some years ago from a scrap yard and it has gone through a myriad of incarnations including a temporary pig (weaner) shelter. Fridges and freezers, especially chest freezers, make extremely good feed containers which is, I suppose, a viable alternative to paying for their disposal. It is possible to make circular bulk feed bins out of corrugated or box section sheet. Run the corrugations up and down and bolt the sheets together through their overlapping edges.

Use a bolt every 30cm from the floor upward. You can make these circular bins with a diameter from three or four feet, right up to tens of feet. To stop rats entering the base of the bin, you need to either cast a plug of three or four inches of concrete in the bottom or bolt the bin to a level floor that leaves no gaps around the bottom edge.

Rat Bait Stations

Following on from how to store vast quantities of ratty grub, here's how to rid yourself of the blighters. Don't bother buying poison from any run of the mill household or DIY shop; it's not generally up to much. Buy your rat poison in plastic buckets from an agricultural merchant: Slaymor springs to mind. Rats will always find the food wherever it is left, but unfortunately so might birds, dogs and kids. Use 18˝ lengths of 4˝ pipe as your bait stations. Carefully place a scoop of poison in the centre of the pipe length and lay it level along a wall or run. The food is out of sight and relatively secure from all but its intended target. Keep topping up your stations, one scoop at a time until the bait stops being taken.

Heated Orphan Lamb Feeder for £25

I've fed several orphan lambs over the last few years and learnt a great deal both about looking after them and the pitfalls of feeding them. When a lamb is born it has a crucial few hours to get a good bellyfull of colostrum; after this time the ability of its stomach to absorb the essential antibodies and proteins from the thick fluid decreases rapidly to nil. It is therefore important that if a newborn lamb has not been able to suck, that it is given replacement colostrum or colostrum hand-milked from another sheep. The problem with many orphan lambs is that they did not get a sufficient dose of the all important colostrum and are therefore weak and have reduced immunity from day one.

33

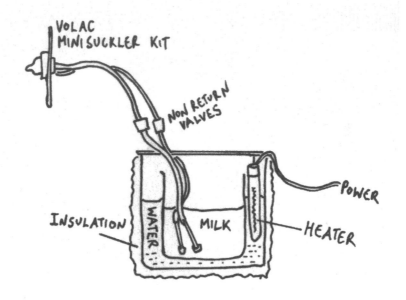

My objective when feeding orphan lambs is to try and replace the mother and keep the lamb growing at a steady rate so that it will eventually be fit for killing. As farmers we are not in the business of running animal charities. Animals should be given a comfortable and humane life up until the point when they are to enter the food chain or need to be culled. The various types and breeds of farm animals do not owe their existence to owners who keep them as pets. I'm not castigating pet owners but it's difficult for many breeds to survive outside of the food chain. Orphan lambs on many farms die because they are not commercially viable but it doesn't have to be like that for the smallholder though.

Initially lambs require four feeds a day but they may show a reluctance to suck and have to be man handled. Some lambs will not suck and require milk 'tubing' directly into the stomach; this exercise is best done under supervision until you are used to it. When lambs are used to feeding, the number of feeds may be reduced to three a day after about a fortnight. Bottle feeding lambs certainly keeps them alive

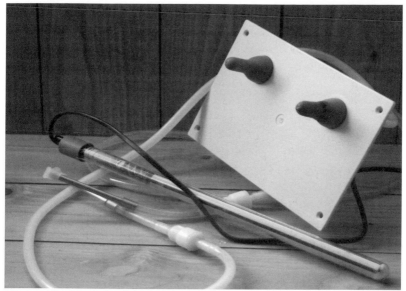

Minisuckler kit and a fish tank heater forms the basis of a heated lamb feeder.

but it has one huge drawback. The lambs often become mis-shapen or 'pot-bellied' and can look like small barrels on legs. Lambs of this nature need to be kept through their first year and into the autumn beyond their first shearing if the best is to be made of their carcase. Eventually they will grow and leave the pot belly behind. The over-riding snag of feeding lambs is that milk replacer costs about £20 a bag and a single lamb could easily need 1.25 -1.5 bags and, at the time of writing, the trade in fat lambs is about £30 a lamb; hardly economical. For the smallholder, however, fattening orphan lambs is worthwhile and is certainly so if you have just a few sheep and sell half-lambs privately, itself a viable and worthy little business.

So, to stop your orphan lambs from going barrel shaped, they will need to self-feed continuously. It's always a downer with sheep farming as heated lamb feeder alone can cost upwards of £150. You can, however, make one for about £30 if you can get your hands on the right bits. Firstly you

35

Build It!

will need a Volac minisuckler kit for an existing 'Volac Ewe 2' feeder. I devised this idea after seeing this kit on the shelves at my local agricultural suppliers. The kit costs about £13 and consists of a plastic plate with 2 removable teats on it. This plate may be tied or screwed to an existing pen or woodwork at the correct height to feed lambs. Try www. cwg.co.uk if nothing is available locally.

Supplied in the kit is enough tubing, non return valves and pick up pipes to marry the setup with a bucket of milk. When the lambs grow on a little, they will readily drink cold milk and so all that would be needed is a plastic food bucket with a tight lid. The lid will require two small holes drilling near to the edge to allow the milk tubes to pass through. Hopefully the proposed method of heating the milk won't be regarded as too controversial but it does work. Heated systems, often at close to £200, contain a 300 watt heater and keep the milk warm at about 30°C. An aquarium heater keeps my fish warm at about the same temperature as the milk and costs about £7. Aquarium heaters are available in a 300w short type (about 8 inches long) and can be purchased in pet shops or on eBay. They contain their own thermostat unit and are adjustable up to about 35°C. The only thing that you must not do is to let them run dry.

Having found a suitably large bucket with a lid, it will require some degree of insulation to stop heat loss – think of the lagging on your hot water cylinder. You could stand the bucket in a box and insulate both around and under it or you could lag your bucket with an old blanket. This first bucket will contain the water which is to be warmed. A second vessel that will hold the warm milk sits inside your contraption. The heater should stand upright and will have a warm water bath around it to keep the milk in the internal bucket warm. Preheat both the milk and the water bath before running the device so that your little heater won't be overworked heating everything up to operating temperature. Aquarium heaters are 240v and are made of glass so they will require a bit of care but they are both sturdy and reliable and you don't hear of many fish owners running into bother with them.

Sheep Feed Troughs

During the winter months, the nutrient level in grass decreases dramatically and what growth there is contains a great deal of water. Hay or silage will keep sheep going through the winter months but as ewes progress through the latter stages of pregnancy, supplementary feed is required to keep the sheep in prime condition and to ensure the continued development of the unborn lambs. Approximately three quarters of the total growth of the unborn lamb occurs within the last eight weeks of pregnancy. During this time the nutritional requirement of the sheep will increase by up to 25% per carried lamb over a ewe that is not pregnant and a sheep that is carrying triplets may need 50% more than a ewe that is carrying just one lamb and 75% more than a ewe that is not pregnant. Ewes that do not get enough nutrient to sustain the development of multiple foetus's will not carry them all to term. Sheep and pigs alike can sacrifice their progeny in the early stages of development if subjected to a lack of food or stress.

Undoubtedly this could all amount to a lot of feed and in the ensuing sheepy frenzy, as you appear outside with a plastic bag, it is all too easy to see the neat rows of pricey grub trampled into the mire. Sheep are usually very peaceful but only until the food arrives. A simple feed trough of a length appropriate to the number of ewes you have will stop any loose feed going to waste and could be made for very little money. As a rough estimate you will probably get 5 or 6 heads around a 3ft trough at the same time and a 6ft trough would have enough space for at least ten moderate sized sheep around it. There are 3 methods of constructing a relatively simple feed trough and one of these is the ultimate

SHEEP FEEDER FROM A TYRE

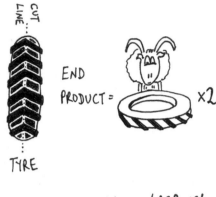

CUT LINE

END
PRODUCT = x2

TYRE

WOODEN 'SPINE'

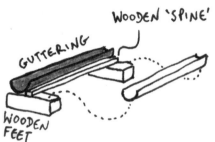

GUTTERING

WOODEN FEET

SHEEP FEEDER
GUTTERING METHOD

in recycling.

Tyre Method

Take one old tyre, the bigger the better; a tractor tyre is ideal. Using an angle grinder with a suitable cutting disc, slice the tyre in half, cutting all the way around its circumference (easier said than done). This will leave you with two circular feeders, both useful for feeding either loose feed or minerals to your sheep.

Guttering Method

Use two equal lengths of the largest width guttering available (typically 112mm). Gutter ends are commercially available to fit but with an electric saw it's a quick task to cut semi-circular pieces that will screw into the ends of your guttering. Find a few lengths of 3 x 2″ or 4 x 2″ to act as feet and cut them to 40cm in length. As guttering is not a very rigid material and may suffer if moved excessively, cut a piece of batten (2 x 1″) or whatever suitable material you have to form a backbone for the trough.

Space out your wooden feet at regular intervals, obviously with one at either end, and screw the wooden backbone down the middle of all the feet. One piece of guttering can be positioned at either side of the backbone piece. Attach the guttering by screwing through the bottom of it into each of the feet; to do this you will need to drill some screw holes first.

Wooden Trough

A traditional wooden trough can be made from three planks of timber, with three blocks for feet and two cut pieces for the ends. It is not advisable to make a trough with a perfectly square profile as sheep will struggle to eat the food that is pushed up against the sides. Like most projects, if you have timber that is available, adapt the design to what you have rather than buying new. If the trough ends up 4 inches deep instead of 5, the sheep won't care. Whatever material you use should be at least 15mm thick, whether it be plywood or softwood.

First make up a couple of ends for your trough as illustrated. You will need three planks, two of 15cm width and one 13cm wide. I would advise fitting the two side planks first, using three screws per side at each end. In the right hand illustration the trough is viewed upside down with one side in place. In order that the bottom panel will sit flush, the protruding corner, as illustrated, needs trimming. Use a plane, a 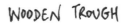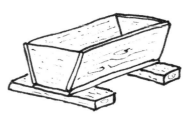 power sander or careful use of a sturdy knife. With some power saws you can set them up to cut a continuous beveled edge.

With the edges trimmed, screw the bottom plank in place. Fit the block feet (as described for the gutter feed trough), securing each one with two substantial screws through the

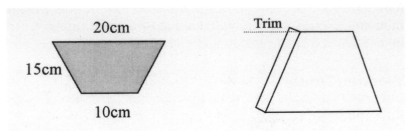

floor of the trough.

Mobile Hay Rack

A flock of sheep around a feeder soon reduce the ground to a soup, so having a feeder that can be moved around is a great asset. Top tip: If you are looking to reseed a particularly muddy piece of ground, then temporarily dispense with any form of hay rack and feed hay loose on the ground. The action of trampling hooves on hay will ensure that the following spring you have a new and luscious green sward where the mud was.

As we all know, decent hay can be costly and therefore the use of a feeder is our only safeguard against wastage. The following hay rack is as simplistic a design as is possible without compromising on strength or longevity. The length of the rack could be adjusted to suit and I suppose that it could be made without the wiggly tin roof if cutting the stuff is not your idea of fun. I shall describe two different ways of building a simple feeder such as this, although I hasten to add that one might look easier to make, but I bet it doesn't last half as long.

Method 1 Basic Mobile Hayrack

Cut two pieces of good quality ply to a size of 60 x 80cm. 19mm would be fine but 12mm would be too thin.

Cut three lengths of timber to the desired length of your rack, in this instance 1m. Anything substantial and above an inch in thickness would do such as 2 x 1″, 2 x 1.5″.

Mark up your side panels to find a central point on each one, 50cm down from what is to be the top edge. This is the position in which one of your 1metre pieces will fit; the remaining two pieces being bracing for the top edges.

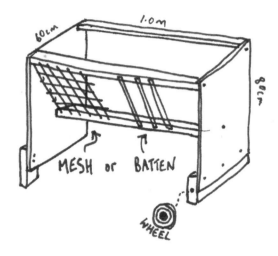

Ideally, the rack will be formed with some suitable 2″ weld mesh. If you do not possess any mesh, you could use 9 pieces of batten per side to form a rack. Screw them top and bottom at 10cm intervals. The plywood ends should not rest on the ground where they will absorb moisture. Screw a block of 3 x 2″ or equivalent to the base of one end that will act as a bearer to which suitable wheels can be attached. The other end should have 2 short legs added later on; the length of the legs will be in relation to the size of the wheels. Obviously it should look level when finished.

The top is generic to both rack designs but if you feel you don't need it, fair enough. Cut some corrugated steel sheet to 70 x 105cm. This will allow for a slight overlap all round for the drips to fall off when it rains. The easiest way to cut

41

Build It!

it is with an angle grinder and a metal cutting disc. It makes a hell of a noise, so do wear all the appropriate safety gear. As an alternative, thin ply or softwood tongue and groove cladding could be used to form a curved wooden roof This should be coated in felt or with a thick treatment.

The roof will need some formers to give it a slight curve; 3 x 1″ or 3 x 2″ would give a slight curve but 4 x 1″ or 4 x 2″ would be better. Cut a 60cm length of whatever it is you have and mark a curve on it, from the bottom left corner of a face, to the bottom right corner of the face, gently brushing the top at the mid point. Cut 2 identical pieces. If you are making a longer rack, you will need at least another one of these to give the roof more rigidity. The last suggestion is not to use a curved roof at all but to make a ridged roof out of two pieces of ply. By running a ridge bar the length of the structure and cutting the ends to an apex, two wooden roofing sheets could be hinged from this ridge piece.

TIN ROOF WITH WOODEN FORMERS

HINGE

Method 2 Mobile Hayrack

An alternate method of building a hay rack is to use all timber and no plywood at the ends. The design is slightly more convoluted, as can be seen in the diagram, but the end result is very satisfactory. Each end of the hay rack can be made from

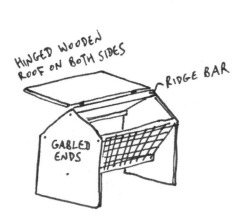

HINGED WOODEN ROOF ON BOTH SIDES

RIDGE BAR

GABLED ENDS

3 x 2″ and the same used for the metre long timber nearest the floor. The top two 1 metre timbers do not need to be so substantial. With many of these projects there are no hard and fast rules. It is simply about making the best use of what you already have lying around. When working with two inch thick timbers, use at least 3″ long screws and drive them until they are slightly sunk into the wood. In this design, made from heavier timber, a combination of screws and nails would work.

You could incorporate a loose feed trough in the lower section of these designs by cutting 2 lengths of previously discussed guttering to fit in the 1m gap. Add a metre long wooden bar for each trough to rest on and screw the guttering to it.

Pig Arks

The cost of buying a pig arc is literally a right swine. They cost a 'pigging fortune' etc. etc. As I breed pigs, there is absolutely no way in the world I'm going to make it pay by shelling out anywhere between £200 and £400 every time I need a new house. It is therefore very cost effective to make pig housing. What you do need to consider, however, is the strength of the pig and you will need to engineer your projects accordingly. A pig will eat your construction. It will also use it as a scratching post and, if it decides that it wants to move the house a little to the left or right, it will do that as well. So build your housing to withstand your pig!

ALTERNATIVE HAYRACK DESIGN

Build It!

Simple but incredibly effective pig arc. Fork in plenty of straw to keep your pig warm in miserable weather

Pig Arc No. 1

This design will accomodate two or three large pigs but could easily be adjusted to house more. I designed my project to use several 5ft lengths of box profile sheeting that I had lying about the place. Box profile steel sheeting is thin and easier to work with than traditional corrugated steel. The initial design did not include a base but this design could easily be adapted to fit to a base mounted on skids. To make this design you will need the following materials:

Two 1.22 x 2.44m (8 x 4 ft) sheets of 22mm exterior ply. Enough 5ft long sheets of 'wiggly tin' to cover a distance of 3.83m with sufficient overlap between each sheet. If you are going to buy new steel sheet, adjust your design to whatever reasonable ready cut lengths you can get.

Timber required will be dependent on the available width of your roofing sheeting; you will need seven 5ft lengths of 38mm² (1½˝). Slightly heavier wood will suffice.

A selection of 3″ and 1½″ screws.

To make a floor you will need an additional 2 sheets of heavy ply, plus 4 lengths of 75 x 50mm (3 x 2″) or 100 x 50mm (4 x 2″) from which skids can be made. If I were making a base for a 5ft deep ark, I would use two

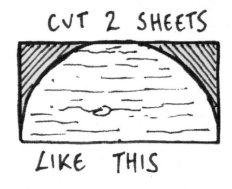

CUT 2 SHEETS

LIKE THIS

pieces of 4 x 2 that were 6ft long for the outer skids and two pieces that were 5ft long and recessed underneath the ark as inner supports.

To make the ark, take the two sheets of 22mm plywood, turn them onto their longest sides and mark a large pencil arc on them. Use a length of string and a pin to make a large compass with which to draw the arc. Find the centre point at the bottom of the long edge and fasten the string here. Tie the pencil in a position on the string so that it just stretches to the top edge of the sheet. Using the taught string as a guide, mark your semi-circle across the sheet. After you have cut them, these pieces of plywood will both be the same size, the largest semi-circles that you could possibly cut out of an 8x4ft sheet of wood. Select the two pieces according to their best grain and note which are to be the insides and outsides. One of the sheets now requires a large, pig sized doorway cutting out. Tailor the size of the doorway to the size of the pig that is to pass through it. If the door is too low, the pig will probably lift the house up as it forces its way in but if the doorway is too large, the pig won't benefit from a draught free house. If you are clueless, make the door 60cm wide and 80cm in overall height. Mark another pencil arc at the top of the doorway in order to cut a nicely rounded tidy opening.

CUT A DOOR TO SUIT
YOUR PIG IN 1 SHEET

Using 3˝ screws and a helper, if you are not a bit of a juggler, fasten the lengths of timber around the perimeter of the ply, screwing from the outside of the house through the ply and into the ends of the timber poles. One piece of timber is positioned at each bottom corner, one as a central roof pole and the rest equidistant in the remaining gaps or else positioned to suit where your overlapped joins of the roof sheeting will be.

If your tin sheets are 5ft long, knock 10cm (4˝) off the length of your 5ft x 38mm² (1½˝) timbers. If you are using 6ft or 8ft sheets, do likewise. This will allow the roofing sheets to protrude over the wooden ark ends and reduce wetness on the edges of the plywood. The metalwork can now be fitted over the skeleton of the house. To do this you will need a strategy for either drilling or puncturing your sheeting to take screws. A large hammer and a suitable nail works. The roof sheets are then screwed to both the wooden frame timbers, and into the edges of the 22mm thick plywood ends. Put a screw at least every 6 inches along each timber and into the plywood.

JOIN THE TWO SIDES TOGETHER
LIKE SO

If you want to build this arc on a wooden base, hold fast on roofing it until the base is made and attached. To make a simple base cut the ends of all your 4 skids to at least a 45 degree slant so they will travel if towed. Use heavy screws to fix the skids to the underside of an 8 x 4 sheet. One 6ft one protruding frontward at each end and two short skids equally spaced underneath. Mark, drill and screw downwards through the floor and into the timbers below. Another 20cm (8˝) strip of the same gauge ply is needed to finish the floor, or more if your design is for a larger pig ark. The finished frame can be mounted on its new sledge base using screws and coach bolts before the roofing is finally added.

FIX ON SHEETING
START AT THE BOTTOM
AND WORK UP

OVERLAP ROOFING

SHEETS LIKE THIS

Pig Arc No 2

I made this design to the specifications required to house two fully grown Kune Kune pigs. This breed of pig originally hails from New Zealand and is often kept as a pet due to its small size and docile nature. Don't be fooled! They are wonderful animals but cannot survive simply as a passing pet fashion. Despite what you may have heard they also taste sublime and produce amazing pork if finished correctly; an ideal smallholder's pig in all respects.

The design of this house would also be ideal for Vietnamese

Build It!

Small plywood pig arc on skids. Also great for kids to play in.

or even just a couple of fattening porkers. It could also be scaled up to suit traditional large breeds. The ark is similar to a large chicken house and relatively cheap to make. It is movable, with an integral base and yet only requires 3 large (8 x 4ft) sheets of 12mm or 18mm external ply in its construction. By economic cutting of the plywood sheets, there will also be enough timber for the roof, floor and ends. Three lengths of 3 x 2″ are needed for the skids and about 10 metres of 2 x 1″ roofing lath for additional internal framework. Start by marking and cutting your three plywood sheets as follows:

Cut the 3 sheets across their length, 1.36m from one end. This will leave two pieces out of each large sheet, one section measuring 1.08 x 1.22m and the other measuring 1.36 x 1.22m. The 1.36m panels are to make the floor and roof. Two of the 1.08m panels are used to manufacture the ends. The other piece is spare. Cut two lengths of 75 x 50mm (3 x 2″) to 1.6m and a third length to 1.36m. These are the skids on which the ark will sit. Mark an angle that will slice a wedge of about 15cm long out of the end of each of the skids. Do not shorten the overall length. Simply cut a suitable wedge off each piece. Screw the skids (from above) underneath one of the 1.36m sheets; put the two longest skids at each outside edge and the shorter skid recessed underneath. The two outer skids will protrude forward of the base.

PIG ARC Nº 2

THE BASE

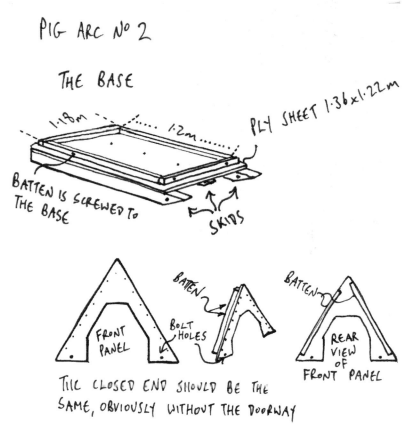

PLY SHEET 1.36 x 1.22m

BATTEN IS SCREWED TO THE BASE

SKIDS

FRONT PANEL

BATTEN

BOLT HOLES

BATTEN

REAR VIEW OF FRONT PANEL

THE CLOSED END SHOULD BE THE SAME, OBVIOUSLY WITHOUT THE DOORWAY

Using 50 x 25mm (2 x 1˝) batten, cut two lengths of 1.18m and two lengths of 1.2m. Fix the 1.20m lengths parallel to the longest sides of the base. Set them 2cm inward of each edge. This should leave 8cm at each end. The remaining 1.18m pieces fit parallel to the short ends of the base. What you are left with is a continuous rectangle of 2˝ wide timber that sits between 2 and 3cm inward from the edge of the base.

Check your three short pieces of plywood for imperfections and decide which pieces will make the best ends and, of those two required sheets, which sides should face inward. Mark and cut the ends so that the grain runs up and down.

Build It!

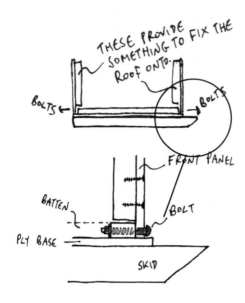

THESE PROVIDE SOMETHING TO FIX THE Roof ONTo.

BOLTS

BOLTS

FRONT PANEL

BATTEN

BOLT

PLY BASE

SKID

Using the 1.22m side as your baseline, find the midpoint and mark it on both opposing edges. Mark another point 1″ down from the centre point of the top edge. Mark your triangular end to this point so that, in effect, it will be close to equilateral (all sides the same length) but not quite. If we were to now measure these triangles, the baseline would be 1.22m but the two other sides should be up to 1cm less.

One of the triangular ends will need to be cut to form a doorway. As pigs come in different sizes, cut it to suit. I doubt that anything less than 45 x 70cm is going to cut the mustard so, if in doubt, measure your pig. It's easy to cut a small door bigger but not the other way round. Cut another four lengths of 2 x 1″ batten at 1.12m length. These lengths are screwed to the inside uppermost edges of the end panels. Screw from the outer side of the panels and use a screw every 15cm. Position the battens so that the 25mm side is against the end panel and the 50mm side can support the roof. Leave a 35mm gap between the bottom corners of the panel and where the battens begin.

The end panels can be presented to the base. Each end should sit snuggly against the batten rectangle that is screwed to the baseboard. The ends are then bolted to this baseboard battening.

This project can be finished with plenty of 25 and 50mm screws. Screws are certainly good, but 60mm coach bolts

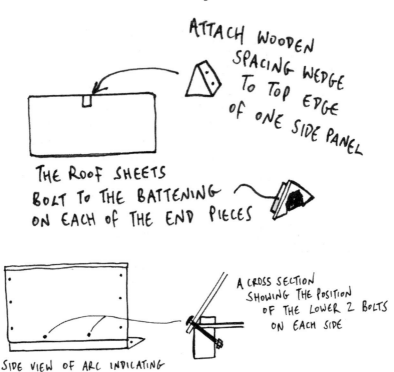

ATTACH WOODEN SPACING WEDGE To Top EDGE of ONE SIDE PANEL

THE ROOF SHEETS BOLT TO THE BATTENING ON EACH OF THE END PIECES

A CROSS SECTION SHOWING THE POSITION OF THE LOWER 2 BOLTS ON EACH SIDE

SIDE VIEW OF ARC INDICATING BOLT POSITIONS ON THE SIDE SHEETS.

and washers are a better bet. You will need 12 coach bolts of about 60mm length, 5 of 75mm length and 4 of 85mm length. Penny washers are also needed to take the load of tightening bolts against soft wood. Fix the ends with screws if you want to, but I will carefully drill 6mm holes and use at least 2 bolts per end, positioned about ½″ up from the base. Once the nuts are tightened, the ends will stand upright unassisted. Before putting the roof on, there is one little extra endeavour I'll describe that will make the job easier. As plywood sheets flex a little, make a spacer out of a wood off-cut that is the same pitch as the roof, using the apex of one of the ends as a template. This triangular piece of 3 x 2″ or similar, need only be 10cm deep, but it will help to brace the centre of the roof. Fit the block to the middle of the top edge of one of your roofing sheets.

Fitting the roof may require two pairs of hands or judicious use of blocks to prop the roof sheets up whilst fixing. The roof sheets are fixed to the battening on the end panels using 3 bolts per end, per side. The roofing panels should slightly overlap the base at their bottom edges to allow water to run off. When you position the second side, the simple function of the wood block in keeping the centre of the top edges apart will become clear. Again, 3 bolts per end and then a screw or two into the top block.

To give the structure some real strength, 2 more bolts are needed per side towards the bottom edge of the roof sheets. By drilling holes in the right position (between 5 and 10cm up from the bottom edge of the roof sheets) it is possible to penetrate the roof sheet, the floor and the skids. A bolt through these holes will lock the lot together. Make these holes about 30cm in from each end of the house. You will need a long drill and, whilst 60mm coach bolts might have worked for the roof, you will need at least 85mm bolts for this job.

Drill a 12mm hole through the front of each of the longer skids to take a tow rope. Apart from painting the structure, the only remaining job is to close off the gap in the roof. This is a pretty low tech affair and in my previous projects has been achieved with a length of 4″ wide plastic damp proof course (any other heavy duty plastic would also do) stapled to the woodwork with standard household staples.

Loose Box/Field Shelter

Buildings such as field shelters that are not on a permanent base and can be moved, fall into a convenient gap in planning law and do not require permission in normal agricultural usage. That said, recreational horses do not generally constitute agriculture and local authorities may not

Panels of the unused and unloved field shelter. The doorway can be seen as can the methods of constructing both framework and cladding.

agree with your argument in these circumstances. Building a simple field shelter is not difficult, but as the quantity of timber required for such a project is not cheap, forethought needs to be given to the planning and contrivance of this idea. First decide whether looks or cost are your main objective. You've got to clad it in something and, whilst shiplap or tongue and groove cladding does look very nice, it costs a great deal more than exterior plywood.

This project is based on constructing four separate panels that can be bolted together to form a 10ft x 12ft shed with a single pitch roof sloping from front to back. The framework is made from 3 x 2″ carcassing and, in its original form, the cladding was shiplap softwood. The idea of constructing panels is neither new nor my own idea, but simply illustrates that by taking things one step at a time, it is relatively easy to build a decent animal shed. Have a go and adjust the sizes to suit your own needs. Start by making the 6 x 10ft back panel as it's the easiest. Cut 2 lengths of 3 x 2″ to 3.05m (10ft) long, and four lengths to 1.73m. Using nails of

Build It!

at least 10cm (4˝)length, assemble the frame as illustrated in the following diagrams. The frame then needs to be clad with your chosen covering. Using shiplap timber, I used a nail gun to pin the exterior woodwork to the frame.

The front and sides are of a similar construction method, but the frames are different. The side frames are both identical but obviously you will need to clad them on their appropriate sides. The side frames can be made using the following cutting list per side and with reference to the diagram:

1 x 3.65m (12´),
1 x 3.71m (12´ 2˝),
1 x 1.78m (5´ 10˝),
1 x 1.93m (6´ 4˝),
1 x 2.083m (6´ 10˝),
1 x 2.235m (7´ 4˝),
1 x 2.39m (7´ 10˝)

Start with the 12ft piece and mark upright positions at 3ft intervals. The pieces are nailed from left to right with the shortest piece at the left side and the longest upright at the right side. The top of each of the uprights will need to be cut slightly so that the final sloping roof timber piece sits flush on top of these uprights. Use the remaining long piece as a straight edge to mark the uprights for cutting; you will end up removing a small wedge from each upright. The long piece will then be nailed on top of these uprights and should sit flush.

The framework for the shed front and doorway will need adjusting according to your own requirements. The dimensions shown in my example will make

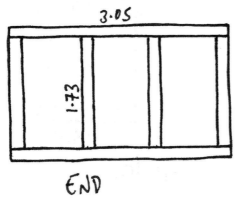

an ideal field shelter for a horse or pony, but you might wish to reduce the doorway size.

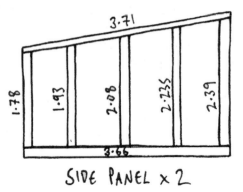

SIDE PANEL x 2

Cut the following pieces of 3x2":
1x 3.05m (10′)
4 x 2.337m (7′ 8″)
2 x 0.915m (3′)
1 x 1.22m (4′)
2 x 0.813m (2′ 8″)

Assemble the front panel as per the diagram and clad with whatever material you are using.

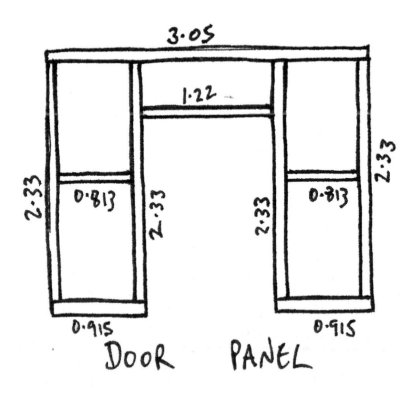

DOOR   PANEL

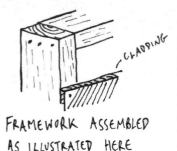

FRAMEWORK ASSEMBLED
AS ILLUSTRATED HERE

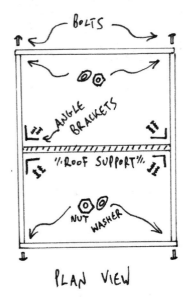

PLAN VIEW

Assembly

You will now have four large, heavy panels and it really is a two person job to put them together. You will need to assemble the panels on a reasonably level surface and must strive to keep the thing square. Three coach bolts are needed per corner, using either 10 or 12mm bolts of 150mm length. Suitable washers will also be necessary. Start by joining the back panel to one of the sides and stand the panels so that the side panel is presented against the inside of the back panel. You will need to drill your bolt holes through the back panel and into the edge of the side panel. The three coach bolts can be tapped through and bolted with washers and nuts and you will need a spanner or a socket set.

Repeat the exercise for the other side panel before attempting to put the front panel in place. Again, make sure that the structure is assembled squarely. The last piece of timber required is a 9′ 6″ piece, needed as a roof support across the middle of the shed. This piece of 3 x 2″ can be held in place with two steel angle brackets and screws at each end. Roofing could be either felted plywood or corrugated sheeting (steel, plastic or bitumen). Treat the finished article with plenty of wood preserver if you want it to last.

Milking machine. The bucket milker and cluster is on the right. The other in-line large bucket prevents milk from accidentally entering the vacuum pump.

Low Cost Milking Machine

Please don't get overly excited because I am not about to show you how to make a milking machine out of nothing. What you may learn, however, is that you can fabricate one, or perhaps even ten, for the same price the manufacturers are demanding for a single cow unit.

When I was in junior school, we lived in a rural farming village where there were probably no less than half a dozen large dairy herds. In the same village these days there are a great many holiday cottages but not a milk cow in sight. Ever wondered what happened to all that milking equipment? Some of it will have been scrapped, but there is plenty still kicking around. My milking machine cost me about £30 to construct and successfully milked Penny Jersey (deceased) for a considerable period of time, eventually outlasting her. The components of a basic milking machine are:

Electric motor, engine or tractor driven power take off. (This provides the rotational force to the vacuum pump).

Vacuum pump – a rotary pump that produces what it says.

Pressure Regulator - in conjunction with a gauge. (This allows variation of the vacuum pressure).

Hoses – formerly all rubber. (Hoses do need to be airtight for the system to work).

Pulsation unit and bucket - takes the steady vacuum and, using a system of pressure chambers and a diaphragm, produces a pulsating rise and fall of vacuum in the line to the cluster.

More hoses.

Claw - this distributes the vacuum to the individual pulsators and also allows the flow of milk back to the bucket.

Cluster - this consists of four individual pulsators, one for each teat.

Rubber liners that fit over the cows teats are fitted inside outer stainless steel sleeves. They use the vacuum to produce a massaging action on the cows teats.

Where to find the parts

I bought my box of bits off eBay for £22. There was even a vacuum pump, although this was not really suited as it needed a flat belt from a tractor or vintage stationary engine to drive it.

These requisite items are usually lying idle in the dusty corners and sheds of most farmers who have been in business for more than 30 years but extracting them may be another matter. As previously discussed, farm sales, eBay and wanted ads are probably the best methods of getting hold of the parts unless you have plenty of farming contacts.

Motors and Pumps

These items come in different sizes and will therefore

require some degree of matching. The general arrangement is that the two items are mounted on a length of steel or timber and are married with pulleys and a belt drive system. A small vacuum pump will produce sufficient draw for one cow with a motor rated at 0.75hp.

A degree of pressure regulation can be achieved by simply having a bleed tap which will allow air to be ingested into the system, thus reducing the amount of vacuum. Too little vacuum and the pulsators will not hold the cows teats, but too much vacuum and the pulsators will be uncomfortable for the cow and may actually damage her teats.

The Bucket Milker

Bucket milkers are still available to buy but, commercially speaking, are regarded as being from a bye-gone era of farming. The milk is collected in an individual bucket that has the pulsation device mounted on top of it. The cluster of pulsators, which are attached to a claw, are connected to the bucket via three tubes. These tubes provide the vacuum to the individual cluster elements and also provide a milk return to the bucket. At one time nearly every farm used these milking devices. As milking parlours progressed, bucket milkers were dispensed with in favour of systems where milk was taken from the cow, put through an individual recording jar and passed on to the cooler and bulk milk tank.

Constructing the machine

Inevitably, working with old milking equipment becomes more of a renovation job than a construction one. Old rubber piping and seals will need to be replaced and the various components stripped, thoroughly cleaned and re-assembled. Pipework on my own machine has been replaced with plastic of corresponding diameters which is available from a local hardware shop off the reel. Plastic cable ties secure the pipework where needed.

Build It!

The vacuum pump and motor. The belt tension is adjustable. The vacuum pump has its own oil reservoir mounted on top of it. This motor is a little on the small side but does suffice for one cow.

Cleanliness is the hardest part of milking a house cow. A cluster, when dropped, becomes a big vacuum cleaner, sucking muck into your nice clean milk bucket. It takes patience and trial and error to learn how to attach the cluster to the udder without it dropping off. If you do not have a scrupulously clean floor, put down a mat or a cover of some sort that the cluster could drop onto. If you have a miserable cow that kicks out, use a kicking bar. We needed to build a rail to restrain the cow because it wouldn't stand still despite being tethered and fed at the same time. The cow was a first time milker, but we won eventually. If you don't want gallons of milk, you can juggle your milking routine with a sucking calf but you will need to have somewhere you can separate the calf for a while so that the cow can bag up prior to milking. Here's my way of operating:

- Start the pump and check the whole unit for sufficient vacuum.
- Clean the cow's teats and grease them a little with some udder cream.
- Bend the short pulsator hoses back around the claw to cut off the suction to each one. Release and attach to the cow, one at a time.
- Hopefully, after a short while, the milk will start to flow. You'll see it squirting through the sight glasses on the top of the bucket.
- Release the pressure from the button on the claw when the milk flow has ceased.
- Apply some more udder cream and pack away.
- Filter and cool the milk as soon as possible.
- Clean, clean, clean – all the gear needs a thorough cleaning job to avoid any bacterial build up.

Build It!

Chapter Three
Poultry Projects

Build your own Chicken Houses

Before you start work on a poultry house, scribble a few diagrams on a scrap of paper and decide on a design for your project. The 3 designs I have trialled have familiar cross sections: rectangle, apex or a box shape with a sloping roof. Box houses are easy to make but don't look particularly attractive. Arks are a great design and lend themselves well to having a run attached, but unless the ark is fairly high, internal space is unfortunately minimised due to the sloping sides. The 'house' cross section is a compromise between the 3 designs; it isn't particularly difficult to make, looks attractive and can be fairly low in height whilst retaining sufficient internal space for the birds.

Build It!

Firstly, decide on how large you want your house to be, I generally build mine to comfortably house trios and quads of birds (approx 2′x 3′). Plan to make your house accessible so that eggs can be retrieved and the house cleaned out without great difficulty. In the summer months chicken houses can become infested by large mite populations that are detrimental to the health of your birds, so 'cleanability' is paramount. Whilst you may be a considerably better woodworker than I and pride yourself on your dovetail joints, don't forget the house needs a certain amount of ventilation.

Timber used to build chicken houses is a matter of personal preference and taste. I have spent £50 on planed timber to build a movable ark with an attached run. I have also completed small houses from cheap fencing material and old plywood for only a couple of pounds. The better quality items may well last longer, although a well made roof will increase the longevity of even the poorest quality wooden box.

The internal 'structure' visible gives something to screw things to.

Constructing a Rectangular House

Start by making the floor of the house. Either a single piece of plywood or pieces of planking will suffice. Create a square of battening on the underside (see exploded diagram). This will provide something of substance to screw the body onto and will also keep the house off the ground, preventing dampness and rot in the floor. If using plywood or other thin materials, the sides of

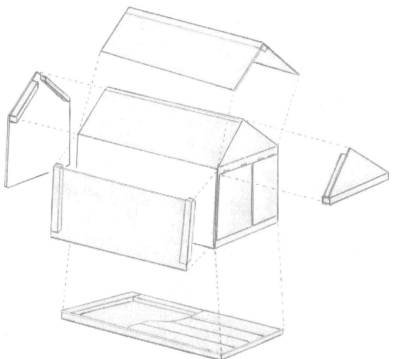

Feather edge boarding under-lined with bitumen felt can form an attractive roof.

the house will need extra upright timbers at the ends to provide a framework onto which the nails and screws can be fixed. Cross members will also give the structure more integrity (refer to the half built photo).

The closed end of the house is fairly self-explanatory and only needs to be carefully measured and cut. The opening end has 2 doors, one of which can be opened for chicken access or both for human access; the missing triangle above the entrances is filled in with plywood. The roof in this instance is created from ply. I have used feather edge fencing timber before, which looks quite nice. The 2 roof sections are screwed to a square baton under the apex giving the roof a 45° pitch. Before the roof is fixed to the house, extra battening needs to be added to the end panels (as rafters) to give something to which one can fix the roof (see diagram).

Inside the house is a full-length droppings tray with attached, raised perches and a nest box area. Hinges for the doors were made from split pins and picture hanging eyes – only because I couldn't face yet another trip to the DIY store. The house was finished with a coat of Ronseal and, as the plywood roof wasn't of great quality, I put some roofing felt on the top.

Chicken Ark with a Run

This was a slightly more advanced project as the construction was designed to be movable and therefore needed some strength. The crux of the job was the framework on which all else fitted. The frame was made from carefully drilled and screwed 45mm² (1¾ inch²) timbers, reinforced with angle brackets at the base corners. The ark flooring was made from plywood and the ark itself was made from shiplap pine cladding, although ply could be used. Additional features to this project included a sliding access door in the side of the ark and removable perches to aid cleaning.

To make an ark and run similar to this that would comfortably house a few hens or four or so bantams, find some timber as previously described and cut 2 lengths of the 45mm² or equivalent to 2m long and one to 2.3m. Cut two other lengths to 1m. Form a 2 x 1m rectangle with the 1 and 2 metre pieces using screws and steel corner braces.

The finished framework. The house and floor are to be built at the nearest end.

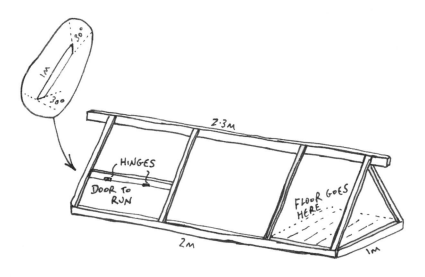

You will now need to cut eight pieces of 1m length to hold the piece of wood that will form the ridge of the run. Mark all of the ends of these 1m pieces and cut a 30 degree

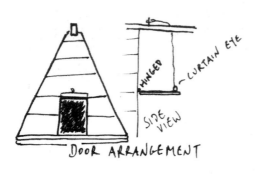

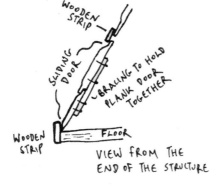

section from each of them as illustrated. The 1m timbers should be positioned and screwed to each corner of the base rectangle with the 30° cuts at the ends allowing them to slant inwards. The topmost 30° cut allows the pieces to butt against the ridge timber. Position another pair about 0.75m in from an end. The remaining pair are positioned at a point about 0.5m from the other end. The ridge timber is then screwed in between these 8 upward and inward pointing timbers. As the ridge timber is slightly longer than the base length, it provides an overlap at each end, which makes a pair of useful carrying handles.

The house can now be constructed around the two sections of the frame that are spaced half a metre apart. First cut a piece of ply or use planking to fit as a floor. Triangular ends need to be measured and cut to fit the structure. One of these will need a door

about 20 x 25cm cutting out of it.
The door is then re-attached with a
hinge at its top edge. By screwing
a curtain eye to the bottom edge of
the door, a string can be attached
with which the door can be raised
and lowered. One side of the
house will need to be either fully
or partially hinged so that cleaning
may take place and eggs can be
collected. It's probably better to
make the bottom 30cm of one side

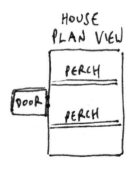

opening along its entire length, although some water may
enter along the hinge line. Alternatively, you could make a
sliding door. Make both of the sides overlap the base slightly
so that the rain and drips run off. Two perches should be cut
to fit and positioned inside the house, one on either side of
the doorway.

The run needs a point of entry for feed trays and water.
This can be made by fixing a horizontal bar 30cm from the
base between two of the upright frames. This will provide
a fixing point for more hinges and another plywood door to
cover the doorway into the run. The project I originally built
using this method was covered in chicken wire which was
fastened to the framework with small staples (the nail variety,
not paper ones). Weldmesh would serve equally well but is
more expensive. The catches I used on this design were of
the turn button variety.

The chickens have given their stamp of approval to these
projects. I would go as far as to say that the oldest and wisest
chicken has a fair idea what's going down every time I set
to with my tools. It's quite amusing to turn over a nearly
finished house for that extra nail and discover that a stealthy
feathered inspector is already inside. Chicken houses can be
built on any budget and to any size size. If the construction is
predator proof and weather proof then your chickens will be

Build It!

Budget chicken arc. The position of the screws on the side indicates the internal partition of the nesting end from the roosting compartment.

just as happy, whether it cost £5 or £50.

Budget Poultry Ark

This design is for a 3 to 4 bird chicken ark. The job should take anyone with a modicum of DIY ability approximately 4 hours to complete. The materials will cost up to £50 depending on where they are purchased and the grade of wood used. This design was conceived to be simple and postable, so it was briefly available on eBay some years back. The plans were also contrived back then and I have left them in their original form. Chicken houses don't get much easier.

Materials and Equipment Required

A decent timber supplier will saw this wood to these sizes for you. Starting with this pre-sawn list will reduce the construction time dramatically.

2″ x 1″ planed -1m	x1
9mm interior quality ply - 1m x 0.6m	x3
18mm ply - 0.52 x 1.2m	x1
18mm Ply - 0.24 x 0.32m	x2
45 x 45mm rough sawn - 0.65m	x3

Screws - 38 brass 7 x 1¼, 8 brass 10 x 2
2 brass hinges
Door bolts/securings

Step 1

Using the 1.2 x 0.52 18mm ply, mark out 3 equilateral triangles as illustrated. The shaded areas are scrap and are not required. The length of all the sides of each triangle should be 60cm. Just 4 cuts are required to create the three triangles.

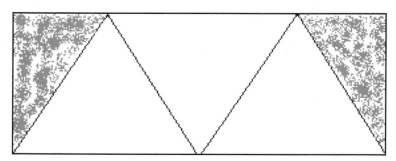

Step 2

All 3 triangles need to have a doorways cut into them. Mark the doorways as shown in the middle diagram. The top curve can be marked with a compass. If you don't possess one, tie a length of fine string to a pencil and a drawing pin; set a length of 10cm.

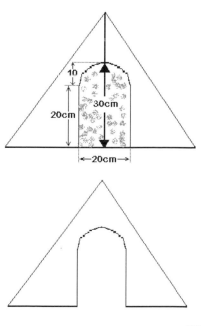

You may find it easier to mark up the doorway after drawing a faint line dividing the triangle in two, from the top apex to halfway (30cm) along the base.

Build It!

After cutting you should be left with three sections of 18mm ply shaped as illustrated below. Small variations in door size don't matter but any variations in overall section will, so take care when both marking and cutting.

Step 3 – The Base

All 3 sheets of 9mm ply (1 x 0.6m) need to have 9 holes drilled in them. The easiest way to do this is to mark and drill 1 sheet and then use it as a template to drill the others. Use a 2mm drill bit. The hole positions are marked with a dot.

Select one of the drilled 9mm sheets for the base. The 65cm rough sawn timbers are to be screwed to the underside of the

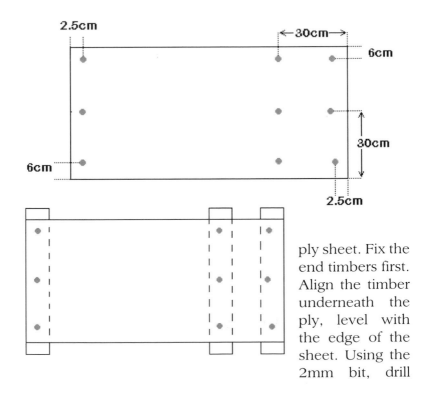

ply sheet. Fix the end timbers first. Align the timber underneath the ply, level with the edge of the sheet. Using the 2mm bit, drill holes into the base timbers using the pre-drilled ply as a guide. Once the wood has been drilled, screws can be used to fasten the supporting timbers to the base sheet.

Step 4 – The Doors

Mark both door pieces as follows and cut off 2 corners

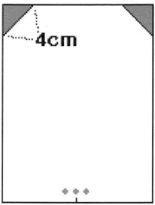

Use a ruler to measure and mark the door edges to accept one large or two small hinges. Drill holes for the screws according to hinge size. If in doubt use the smallest bit possible; you can can make the holes bigger later on.

The doors are attached to the base as illustrated below, one at each end. The edge of the base will need to be marked and drilled correspondingly.

Note the hinge position in the above diagram. What you should end up with is the arrangement illustrated over the page.

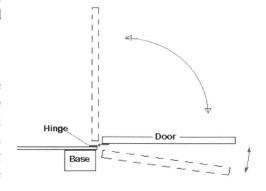

Step 5 – Adding the Roof

Warning – assemble this project on a level surface or you will find it difficult to achieve a quality finish. Have a good

Build It!

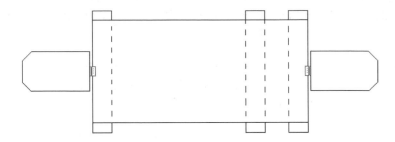

look at the 3 triangular doorway sections and select the two pieces which have the best faces to be the visible (exterior facing) ends of the Ark. The remaining middle section should be attached first.

Align the middle section above the timber support (30cm in from the end) as illustrated in the above left diagram. Ensuring the pre-drilled holes are in the correct place, rest a 9mm ply sheet against the door section, as illustrated in

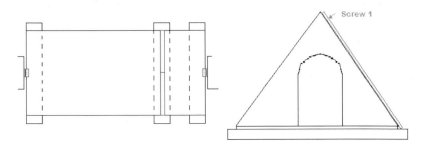

the above diagram. The sheet should rest on the protruding floor support timbers from underneath the base.

Using the pre drilled holes in the roof sheet as a guide, drill a hole into the carefully positioned doorway and fix with a screw (shown as screw 1 in the above diagram). With a first screw in place, aligning and drilling the remaining holes becomes slightly easier.

Repeat this process for the other 2 doorway sections on side 1. When side 1 is secure, follow the same procedure for side 2.

When all the screws are in place, the roof structure is secured to the base by drilling a 3mm hole through the ply and into the base timbers and securing with the long screws.

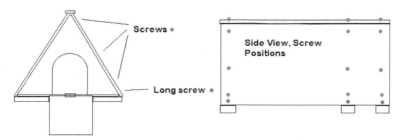

The roof capping bar can be added next. Carefully saw off the protruding, exposed points of the doorway sections.

Holding the roof bar in place, mark the position of the doorway sections onto it and drill 3 holes in the appropriate places. Screw the capping bar in place.

Door Catches

Door catches are a matter of personal preference. Hooks and eyes are inexpensive and easy to fit but bolts require a little more work. The simplest method is as follows:

Use a long screw for the pivot.

2.5cm

Build It!

Perches

Removable perches are easy to make and any suitable scrap timber can be used, including old tree branches.

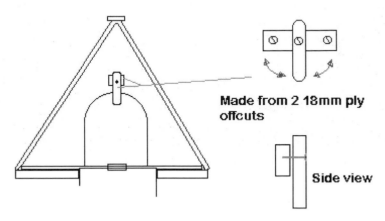

Made from 2 18mm ply offcuts

Side view

Saw a 50cm length of suitable perch material. A 2-4cm wide x 2cm thick offcut or a 3cm diameter stick is ideal. Mount it on 15 x 6 cm blocks. Drill and screw at each end.

Treatment

In order to prolong the life of timber kept outside, suitable treatment must be used. From past experience, some of the expensive wood treatment products require re-application almost yearly and do not last as long as standard outdoor paints. Ensure any paint or treatment is worked into the edges where the majority of damaging water penetration will occur.

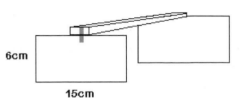

6cm

15cm

A door at each end facilitates cleaning and egg removal.

Fox Proofing

If you live in an area that is persistently plagued by foxes then unless you take great precautions you are most definitely going to lose poultry. I have been there. The trouble is that once a fox knows where your chickens are, they may even fancy their chances in the daytime. It is possible to fox proof chicken buildings to a degree, but it does not protect against the downright implausible. There are many farmers wives' tales of how to keep the fox at bay. Some of them actually work but most don't. Perhaps the most important common sense rule is to make sure that, come dusk, the house and run doors are secure. Although foxes will often watch your flock from the safety of a hedge in broad daylight, they are generally more wary in daytime than when under cover of darkness. On odd occasions there has been no one around to shut the doors of my hen houses at dusk. My remedy has been to leave plenty of lights on. A flood light in the yard and leaving the conservatory lights on seems to work for me. The one time I didn't leave any lights on at all a chicken was taken. Unfortunately foxes do get used to permanent lighting so if you rely on the same stationary outside light every night as a fox deterrent, you can forget it. The fox certainly will.

Fencing

The first real line of defence for chickens is a sturdy house with a secure door. A run is generally only in use during the day. Although it may be secure and the mesh dug a foot into the ground to prevent burrowing, it won't always stop birds being killed. Foxes may even try to climb fencing and runs are best covered with a sturdy top unless the sides are 6ft or above in height. Recently a friend lost a very expensive ornamental pheasant. A fox climbed on top of the run and panicked the bird into flying upward, trying to escape. The fox had head of pheasant for tea whilst the body remained in the run. You just can't protect against that. Stout framework, secure nails and galvanised chicken wire still remain at the technological forefront of economical chicken protection.

Electric fencing

In my experience the best method of protecting against larger predators is electric fencing. Many people have preached about the need for only a single strand of electric wire at a low height of around 8 inches from the ground, about 2 feet away from the main chicken wire fence. Although I haven't tried this method I am aware that it is successful and is a cheaper alternative to my own preferred method.

Electric poultry netting is a real boon in the field of chicken keeping. The only thing it does not protect against is the particularly flighty bird that doesn't want to stay in the enclosure. Available in 25 or 50 metre rolls, it costs from around £50 for 50m from farm suppliers and farm co-ops, which is roughly the same as chicken wire. With a bit of judicious planning, one large roll of electric net can be used

Electric poultry netting keeps birds in and foxes out.

to construct 2 or 3 adjacent runs on a suitable swathe of grass. The price even includes poles every 5 metres or so, although a few extra are required to make a really sturdy fence. Coupled with a suitable electric fencing unit, electric netting keeps the birds in and most other stuff out.

Chick Brooder / Growing Box

The natural way of rearing chickens is to find a broody hen to sit on some eggs for you. They do say that nature's ways are best, however from a vaguely financial point of view I don't tend to agree. Whilst I appreciate that some of my hens try to be good mothers, they simply cannot compete with the rats, stoats and hedgehogs that snipe at their little gangs of fluffy followers. Having at the time of writing had a scurrilous year in terms of numbers reared by hens, I have to concede that artificial chicken rearing is the only way I can replenish my stocks. After hatching the chickens in an incubator in my lounge, they are transferred into plastic

Build It!

storage containers where they bask for a week or two under a heat lamp. After a few days the chicks usually begin to stink the room out and my wife starts to moan. In the spring it is often still too cold to keep the chicks outdoors, even with a heat lamp. Whilst we do have outbuildings, it is problematic keeping young chickens away from the local rat population and so I choose to keep them in a large high sided brooder box in a shed.

The first brooder run I built was made from some discarded plank doors and lasted 5 years before being burnt. This first experiment measured approximately 5ft x 2ft and was very successful in that it could be used outdoors as a stand alone item. One end of the run was completely enclosed and had a removable, watertight felt roof under which the heat lamp could be safely attached and remain on come rain or shine without cooking the young chicks. As a quick aside on heat lamps, they generally come in the 250 watt size. Unfortunately, these large bulbs use 6 kilowatt hours per day of electricity which ends up costing about £5 a week. For the small poultry breeder this size of bulb is really overkill. Writing as someone who keeps pigs and such like, I often end up running several such devices at once and it can be seen how quickly large electricity bills will mount up. In a confined and draught free environment, I have found that normal household reflector bulbs in a proper metal heat lamp shade work adequately well. Dependent on the number of chicks, 80w or 100w bulbs will suffice. It is also possible to mask the light output to a degree using large metal cake or biscuit tins. After Christmas, an empty Roses or Quality Street tin can often be found and these are useful for making dull heat emitters for rearing poultry. Heat lamps can occasionally be found in a 150watt size, although they are like the proverbial hen's teeth in my part of the world. If you ever see them for sale snap up a couple quickly.

To build a very simple 4 x 2 x 2ft brooder box that can be used indoors, get a large sheet of plywood; 12mm ply would do but 18mm will be better. Exterior grade (the cheapest) is fine. A single sheet of ply measures approximately 1.22 x 2.44 m or 8ft by 4ft in old money. By some simple maths, if you cut your sheet across its width three times at regular intervals, you will end up with 4 pieces of 2 x 4ft ply. Cut one of these 2 x 4ft lengths in half to form the two box ends. Both ends will need a strip of wood trimming off one edge. If using 18mm ply, cut off a 36mm strip but if using 12mm ply cut off a 24mm wide strip. The three remaining 2 x 4´ lengths will form the base and two sides of the box. By using a fine drill (2mm) and some 30 - 35mm length screws,

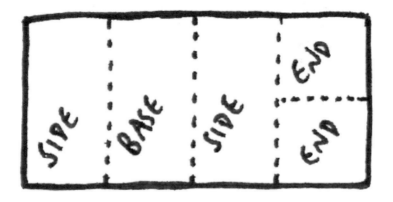

you can assemble your simple box as per the illustration.

The top of the box will need a piece of wire mesh or chicken wire to stop the young birds flying upwards and out. The heat lamp can be suspended above the wire mesh. In a previous incarnation of this project, I chose to partially enclose the top of the box with another piece of plywood so that the young birds had an area to hide out of the way of the heat lamp. When you finally get to set the thing in motion, use either wood shavings, sawdust or even dry sand as a medium for absorbing droppings. A regular scattering of your chosen medium will also ensure that the birds have something to scratch around in and that they won't get their new feathers soiled.

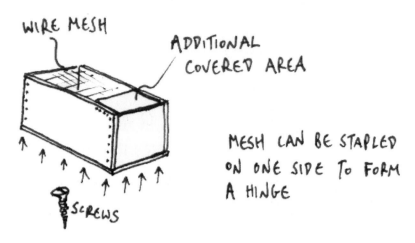

WIRE MESH

ADDITIONAL COVERED AREA

MESH CAN BE STAPLED ON ONE SIDE To FORM A HINGE

SCREWS

Chicken and Rabbit Proof Fencing

It seems fit at this point to add a section on how to fence poultry out of an area. The great problem with keeping chickens is that it is impossible to mix them with my wife's pursuit of vegetable gardening. No sooner has the fork touched the soil than the flock arrives to help. On the few occasions where they do not spot gardening work going on, they do feel it necessary to give the plot a second digging after you have gone inside for a cup of tea. Whilst that is all well and good, the seeds and bulbs that have just been carefully planted are dug up, pecked and strewn all over the place. Seedlings are a prime target for both poultry and woe betide anyone who thinks that their brassicas will survive to see a crop. They most certainly will not. The other problem that many of us are faced with is rabbits. During the growing months, it is possible to contain poultry to a degree but rabbits are a different matter. I usually manage to keep the nearest rabbit warrens sanitised during veg time but in the summer one only has to rest the gun for a couple of weeks and the warrens are soon occupied again.

Having gleaned many fencing tips over the years for keeping these sorts of unwanted pests out of gardens, I have

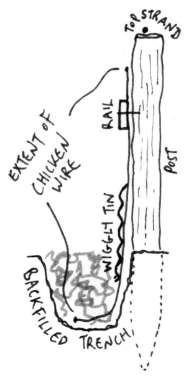

A CROSS SECTION
THROUGH THE
CHICKEN / RABBIT
PROOF FENCE

developed a system that suits my own holding. The science behind the plans is drawn from the various ideas I've read and seen, but do make your own alterations as you see fit.

To make a fence such as that described here, you will need sufficient fence posts for one every six foot of your fence, 12ft wooden rails, a roll of chicken wire, fencing staples, a roll of galvanised top strand wire and some corrugated or similar sheeting. Start your fence by digging a trench about a spade's width and a spade's depth all the way around the area to be fenced. Lay out a line by which you can position your fence posts every 6 foot. The posts should be driven in along the inside (garden side) line of the trench. Use a steel point bar to make pilot holes into the ground before banging your posts in. The chicken wire is unrolled and fastened to your fence posts. Be sure to keep it straight, neat and taught, which is easier said than done. The bottom edge of the chicken wire is to be buried under ground in your trench. Lay the chicken wire so that it is laid flat and covers the bottom of the trench and curves upwards at the base of the fence posts. The reasoning behind this is that when a rabbit tries to dig under the fence, it will not find the bottom edge of the wire, but will simply dig down into a fold of wire netting. The strength of the fence is improved by adding rails to it, although they should be positioned so that there is a good 8″ of wire netting above them. If one were to position the rails at the top edge of the netting it would simply give the poultry something to perch on. When a chicken prepares to launch itself skyward, it does a quick risk assessment of what it is intending to perch on. Chickens struggle to judge the distance of wire, string and fine netting, which clearly serves as a useful deterrent. Run a tight galvanised wire along the tops of all your fence posts. The fence posts themselves can be protected from perching by either cutting them to a fairly sharp point or by adding a selection of suitably long nails protruding at jaunty angles.

The addition of at least a 0.5m depth of metal sheeting all the way around the base of the fence doesn't look particularly appealing visually, but it is effective. The old adage "What the eye doesn't see, the heart doesn't grieve over" is very apt. The tin work stops most poultry (unless you have Jersey Giants, which are so heavy they can't get off the ground anyway) from seeing what is growing on the other side of the fence. It also has the same effect on rabbits, although I suspect they can smell juicy veg from a mile away. Lastly, backfill your trench and compact the soil as best you can to minimise the chances of immediate re-excavation.

Does it work? Quite simply yes, it does! We have successfully constructed two separate veg patches to this specification. In the year of writing there were no known chicken incursions, although there were signs of numerous aborted burrowing attempts. The gateway to our most recent patch was built from a piece of polycarbonate sheet that rested snuggly against the ground. This was obviously less secure than a decent gateway but was in the same spirit as the fencing. A piece of tin or suitable woodwork should be fastened across the bottom foot of the gateway giving a barrier that can be stepped over but not seen through at ground level. Chicken wire still needs to be dug in across the gateway as described earlier or else the fence will have a vulnerable point. If preferred a decent gate could be constructed to fit in the gateway above the ground level barrier.

Fort Brassica. The veg stays inside, the rabbits and poultry remain out.

Our vegetable patches built to this specification have one other utilitarian objective that I have not as yet disclosed. By the addition of an internal rail about 6 inches high and occasionally, on an individual case basis, an internal strand of electric wire, these well fenced plots can easily house small pigs, weaners or growers. Pigs dig up the garden, manure it and make use of all the old vegetable stalks and root systems.

Some types of poultry, especially the bantam breeds, fly remarkably well and it doesn't matter how much fencing you erect, you are never going to contain them completely. If you build a fence system such as this and are still getting regular bird visits, try growing your veg under cloches until it is well past the seedling stage.

Build It!

A Word on Creating Larger Poultry Houses

For those with an interest in keeping larger numbers of hens for egg laying purposes, I often marvel at the prices that are charged for chicken sheds that will house more than ten or fifteen birds. Further on in this epistle is a commentary on building pig arks which could easily be adapted for housing larger quantities of chickens. I have, on occasion, seen fairly robust little garden sheds for sale in the DIY stores for as little as £99 that could also easily be modified into poultry houses suitable for more than 20 or 30 hens. As all poultry housing is best made movable to save spoiling areas of grass or pasture, suitable transport adaptations can easily be made to existing sheds. Using 4 x 2″ or other equally heavy timber, make up a set of skids for an existing shed or, alternatively, a wooden sub-frame that will allow a set of wheels to be attached. By effectively making a timber sledge you could soon have a large and movable chicken shed on the cheap. Perches can be made easily out of wooden laths or battens looking something like a four or five foot wide ladder with only four or five rungs (perches). You will enable a maximum number of birds to use the perching space by positioning this arrangement at a 45 degree angle so that its feet are fixed to the floor, but the ladder top is resting against one of the shed walls.

Nesting Boxes

Chickens do like to lay their eggs with a little privacy so you will have to create some sort of a nesting area or box to which they can retire for this purpose. On smaller poultry sheds and arks, it is enough to let them use the dark area at the back of the house as long as the bedding is changed regularly. For larger sheds you will need to make your own nest boxes. Make a box out of plywood using the same technique as described in the brooder box construction. Use the full width of a ply sheet and cut from it three 4 x 1ft pieces. You will also need

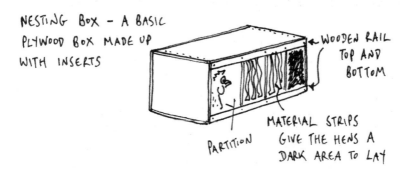

NESTING BOX - A BASIC
PLYWOOD BOX MADE UP
WITH INSERTS

← WOODEN RAIL
TOP AND
BOTTOM

MATERIAL STRIPS
GIVE THE HENS A
DARK AREA TO LAY

PARTITION

5 pieces of 1ft² for the ends and internal partitions. Assemble your box with suitable screws, adding the partitions as a last job. The box will lie on its side when in use. The top and bottom edges of the box should have an additional length of wood added. The lower strip will stop eggs rolling out and the upper strip will give something to attach curtaining to. The final addition is a 4ft long piece of material that will screen the openings to each laying compartment. Cut the material to size and staple it in place to the wooden rail at the top. The material will need to be slit every 5cm or so to permit the chickens to push their way through the screen.

Build It!

A National beehive in action. Note the protective clothing and smoker. A perforated mouse guard is fitted over the entrance indicating that this inspection was early on in the year.

Chapter Four
Beekeeping Projects

From medieval times until around a hundred years ago, bees in the UK had generally always been kept in straw skeps. The main problem with using this method of beekeeping is that it is not possible to carry out manipulations of the colony and in many cases the bees were simply destroyed in order to harvest the honey crop. It was not until 1851 that a US beekeeper discovered the bee space; the naturally occurring separation between vertically hanging combs that the bees build and work in. This discovery by the Reverend Langstroth, enabled the development of a beehive where all the combs were built within movable wooden frames. This meant that individual combs of bees could be removed from the hive and examined. This newfound ability to manipulate bees effectively meant that they could then be managed in a

Build It!

Author's bleak windswept apiary with sheep proof fencing.

way that could maximise honey production. Archaeological evidence has shown that the ancient Greeks did employ a method of using movable combs in bee hives but, like many things, these methods were lost down through the ages.

Unless you have a problematic medical condition or are allergic to bee stings, you can keep bees. Colonies of bees are often kept in unusual locations, sometimes with very limited space available. Contrary to popular belief, European bees do not go out of their way to sting people and if a clear flight path is available they will take it. I have a colony of bees relatively close to my house which as yet have not been problematic. There are instances of people living in flats keeping bees but before going down this route and removing any roof-tiles to provide the bees with a new doorway, do check with the owner first!

Keeping bees in a small garden or yard, either in the town or country, can be very successful if the correct management techniques are employed. Don't go removing the hive roof with your neighbour watching closely over the fence; he won't thank you for it. The varieties of flora and fauna in many towns do make them an ideal habitat for bees. The modern day proliferation of trendy gardeners and year round cultured flowers gives the bee plenty of foraging choice.

Many beekeepers do not keep their bees on their own property. Out-apiaries are often sited on farms, in fields and orchards and the promise of a few pounds of your quality honey can be a great deal maker when looking for a site.

When I first started investigating beekeeping I thought that I would go on the internet, buy a couple of books and hey presto, I would have enough information to go and find some bees. In retrospect I would not recommend this. It may be that somebody else has offered to teach you how to keep bees or it may be that you live so far from anywhere that you cannot find anyone else nearby who is interested. I would suggest that you at least try and find someone who is prepared to let you get your hands dirty for an afternoon. Beekeeping sounds great in practice but the sight of 50,000 angry bees in the air can be slightly daunting and might not be for you. Think hard before you spend your money! If a knowledgeable friend offers you help take it but make sure that your mentor is up to date on aspects such as disease prevention and control. The chances are that, unless they are in regular contact with other beekeepers, they won't be. I recently spoke to someone who had kept bees for several years (but not recently) and they claimed to know a great deal about beekeeping but they knew very little about the treatment and management of varroa, a prevalent and potentially catastrophic modern pest. Don't turn offers of help down but be aware that you might not be getting 100 percent of the picture. There are still many people who think that they can keep a box of bees at the bottom of the garden and, with minimal interference, reap the benefits. This practice of 'bee ownership' rather than beekeeping is unwise. Bee ownership encourages the spread of disease, colonies do not produce their full honey crop potential, nuisance bees are lost to swarming, breeding is not selective and may produce poor strains of bees and eventually your colony will die out anyway. So please, either keep bees or don't.

Build It!

If you cannot find anyone who is prepared to help on a practical basis then a decent pile of books is a must. Recommended reading and probably THE textbook on beekeeping is Hooper's Guide to Bees and Honey, available from most beekeeping suppliers and probably on order from most bookshops. By far the easiest, the most inexpensive and the most enjoyable way to start beekeeping is through a club or association. Most associations are affiliated to the British Beekeeping Association (BBKA) (www.britishbeekeepers.com) and being a member of this association has the added benefit of newsletters, insurance and various other worthy items. By making initial contact with your local association secretary you will be able to find out about events, lectures and practical sessions that your club may have planned for the forthcoming season.

Simple Top Bar Hive

In their natural environment bees choose to live in hollow trees, cracks in rock outcrops etc. The environment that human beings have created has given bees a whole new variety of places to live such as roof spaces and church steeples to name but two. In a natural colony of bees, the colony expansion is generally sidewards. In a hived colony, we artificially force the brood nest (where the bees are born and bred, so to speak) to expand upwards once it has filled its immediate chamber.

In Africa and many other parts of the world where expensive beekeeping equipment is not available, top bar hives are the most common method used to farm bees. They can be very easily constructed and maintained and, if well fashioned, will also suit a western climate. In a top bar hive the combs are movable with care but are only attached to a wooden top bar and not enclosed in a full frame. This has some drawbacks. During a honey flow the hive could easily become full up. As you cannot readily add extra space as you can with other hive designs, you will need to remove honey combs as and when extra space is needed. Lastly, if you gain a colony of very prolific bees, they may soon expand to fill the box. Swarm control is beyond the remit of this book but it does need serious consideration as it is not directly possible to add more space to this hive. However, that is not to say that something could not be adapted or invented to allow colony expansion. Honey production with a top bar hive is generally considered to be less than with conventional hives.

One positive advantage to working one of these hives is that the top bars form a lid on the brood nest; in a conventional hive the bees are exposed once the crown board is removed. It follows, therefore, that by only removing one comb at a time for inspection, there is less upset and disruption to the bees as they are not all exposed to the light. Because of this, the number of flying bees during an inspection should be considerably reduced.

Bearing in mind that the hive and its contents will sit outside all the year round, do build with longevity in mind. Use at least 12 or 18mm exterior grade ply but, if you can afford it, use marine ply.

When constructing a top bar hive, there really is only one dimension of the design that needs to be critically adhered to. The width of the top bars cannot be adjusted as it is calculated in relation to the previously discussed bee space. That dimension is 1⅜″ or 35mm. This design will make a hive with 25 top bars and, by some rudimentary mathematics, you can adjust your hive to be longer with more bars if you wish.

Cut the following panels of plywood:

2 sides – 90 x 30cm
Roof – 100 x 55cm

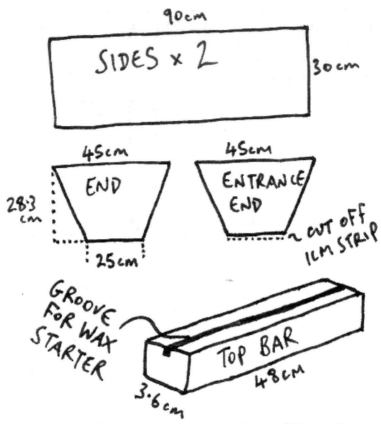

Floor – either 25 x 91.5cm or 2 sections of 25 x 20cm and the remainder in 2-3mm mesh floor
End – cut from a 45 x 28.3cm piece

In addition, 25 top bars are needed. These need to be cut carefully at 36mm wide and 480mm long. Ply is not really the right material for top bars so use softwood between 15 and 25mm thick.

First cut the two ends as per the prescribed diagram. Once you have done this, take one of the end pieces and cut an additional 1cm off the bottom (shortest) edge. This shortened end panel now leaves a space for the bee entrance underneath. Assemble the hive using either screws or a combination of glue with suitable pins or nails. Join the longer of the two hive ends to the hive floor first. Consult the diagrams and ensure that the panel is mounted against the end of the floor and not on top of it.

If you are using shortened floor panels and a mesh floor centre, join one of the 20cm floor panels to the hive end as described above. As you add the two sides to the hive you will see that your full length floor extends past the sides. At the entrance end of the hive the protruding floor forms an alighting board for the bees to fly from. If you are constructing a mesh floor, add your second ply floor piece and leave it sticking out 2.5cm further than the end of the side panels. Position the plywood hive end between the two sides and the floor panel. As this panel was cut down a little, when it is fixed in place it should leave an entranceway for the bees that measures some 25 x 1cm.

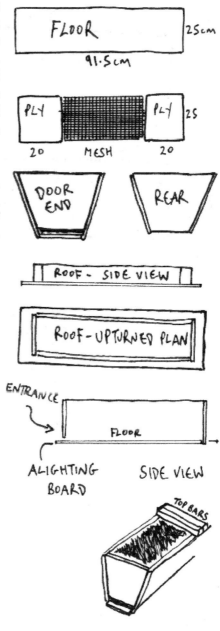

Build It!

A National hive floor that has been doctored to take wire mesh.

If you are fitting a central mesh floor it can now be attached.

Mesh floor or not?

In the early 1990s a parasitic mite was first discovered in the UK, having worked its way slowly from Asia to Europe. This mite, known as varroa, has decimated European honeybee stocks. Methods of control are usually a mixture of chemical and procedural processes. The addition of the mesh floor is a technique employed to rid the hive of a small percentage of the host mites as and when they naturally drop from the bees. Some colonies cope very well and some actually improve with the extra ventilation in the hive created by a mesh floor but others do not. Hive floors can be dirty places full of dead moths, mites, wax, pollen and other hive detritus. Some colonies are dirty but others try to keep the place clean. In a conventional hive you can change the floor, an exercise which should be carried out yearly. In a top bar hive you will need to transfer the bee stocks to a spare hive in order to give the existing one a clean out.

The top bars will all need to have a grove cut into their underside into which a wax starter strip can be attached or some wax melted. The bees will use these starter strips as a template from which to start building their own comb system. If the bars are not positioned in the correct place, the bees will build the combs to suit themselves. Remember the text on bee space.

Did you know that wax is secreted from glands in young bees?

The roof of these types of hive is often just a sheet of wood or similar to prevent rain entering between the top bars. The problem with the UK is that it's often very windy. Conventional hives have heavy rooves but even so may still require a rock on top to keep the lid down. The top bar hive will most definitely need a weight on it throughout the winter.

Although a simple wood sheet would suffice, do add some battening or other timber around the underside edge of the sheet. This addition could be up to an inch thick but should be deep enough to be below the level of the top bars. Some lengths of 50 x 25mm (2 x 1 or 2 x ¾") timber would work well, but use what's available.

Budget National Bee Hive

There are a great many designs of beehive; some are quite complex but others such as the top bar are simple. All were designed to suit the particular requirements of the inventor. Some hives have become standards while others have drifted into obscurity. The most common hive in use throughout the UK with both hobby and amateur beekeepers is known

Build It!

as the National beehive.

At this point it may be worth examining the architecture of a movable comb beehive. The hive consists of several parts that rest on top of each other with no universally accepted means of adhesion other than gravity and propolis, propolis being a tree resin that the bees use as a glue. Starting from the ground we have the hive floor. It is either solid or constructed with a fine wire mesh centre. Above the hive floor we have what is known as the brood box where the colony lives and rears its young. Above the brood box is a wire or zinc slotted queen excluder. This device stops the marginally fatter queen bee from ascending into the honey storage boxes (called supers) which are above the excluder. The number of supers on a hive is dependent on the vagarious nature of the honey flow; in winter and spring there may be no supers at all on a hive. If there is a lot of nectar coming in, the bees will soon fill up a super and you will need to put additional ones on the hive. The super is topped with a crown board and on top of that fits the roof.

A National hive measures $46cm^2$. Inside the hive are movable frames onto which sheets of hexagonally imprinted wax foundation are fixed. The bees draw out this impregnated foundation into the familiar hexagonal combs. There are 11 deep frames in the brood box and 11 shallow frames in the supers. The frames are best purchased rather than made and are are not expensive. Frames are spaced to the correct bee distance apart using plastic push-on ends or by seating them in a metal castellated positioning strip that's fitted to the brood box or super.

Commercially available beehives are made from cedar which looks good, weathers well and is long lasting. I've tried oak which also looks good and weathers well but is too damn heavy to lift.

NATIONAL HIVE FLOOR

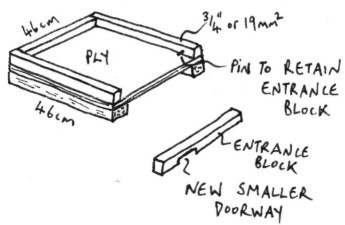

46cm

PLY

46cm

3¼" or 19mm²

PIN TO RETAIN
ENTRANCE
BLOCK

ENTRANCE
BLOCK

NEW SMALLER
DOORWAY

Floor

In the spirit of economy, I'll suggest once again using the best grade of plywood that you can afford. 18mm is better than 12mm and will be used for this design. You will also need some softwood of about ¾" or 19mm² in dimension and something a little more substantial to reinforce the base. I'd suggest buying a piece of 19 x 38mm (¾"x 1.5") roofing lath and thinning it down to size. If you have a good local wood yard they may well have a better selection available.

Let's start by making the base. Carefully mark and cut a piece of ply to 46cm² and cut three pieces of wood (19 x 38mm or even 25 x 38mm) to fit around the underside edge. Fix these in place as per the diagram. Cut three pieces of 19mm² timber to fit around three sides of the top of the base.

To turn this into a simple varroa floor, cut out a central square in the floor, leaving 2 inches around the edges for strength. Fix appropriately sized mesh over the hole in the floor.

Build It!

Entrance Block

During certain times of year and when a colony is weak, an entrance block is needed. This closes down the hive entrance to a size that the bees will be able to manage defensively. Use a piece of 19mm² wood that fills the length of the floor entrance. Use a saw to cut an entrance that is about 50mm long and 7mm deep out of the length of entrance block. You can stop the block being accidentally pushed back into the hive by nailing two pins into the sides of the hive floor. Put the block in position and put pins behind the block at either side, these pins are fixed into the sides of the floor.

Brood box

Working from the floor upwards let's now consider the brood box. A brood box is 225mm deep. Using 18mm ply, cut two pieces of ply 460 x 225 mm. Cut another 2 plywood pieces 424 x 208mm. You will also need:

2 x 424mm lengths of 25 x 38mm (1 x 1 ½"). Any similar timber would work equally well but one of the dimensions does need to be 25mm.
2 lengths of 12mm² or ½"² cut to 424mm.
2 more 424mm lengths of 38 x 12mm (1½" x ½")

You will also need some plastic or metal frame runners – these are inexpensive but could probably be substituted with a little ingenuity. Hopefully you will appreciate that most hive designs were originally done in imperial measurements and the designs don't lend themselves easily to alteration of overall internal and external sizes because these equipment sizes have now become a beekeeping standard.

Assemble the hive on a level surface using glue and 38mm (1½") fine nails. First assemble the basic box shape. The two shorter side panels are both positioned one inch inward of

NATIONAL BROOD BOX

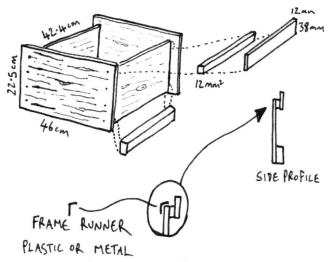

SIDE PROFILE

FRAME RUNNER
PLASTIC OR METAL

their respective ends. This should be clear in the diagram. They will also not be as high as the largest panels. You must take care to ensure that the hive is assembled squarely.

The two bottom bars (25mm^2 or inch^2 softwood) should be glued and nailed in place externally. The woodwork to be done at the top of the two shortened sides is a little less obvious. First fix a ½inch^2 piece of wood flush with the top edges of both the shorter sides. If using nails, it may be worth drilling fine pilot holes in the ½inch^2 wood so that the pins don't split the piece.

Add a piece of 38 x 12mm (1½ x ½″) wood to each of the two short sides, as indicated in the diagram. This piece is positioned against the previously mounted ½″ strips; it is fixed so that it is flush with both the top edge and exterior extremities of the finished brood box.

Queen excluders are not something people generally try to make. You can purchase them online from beekeeping suppliers. Thornes of Wragby (www.thorne.co.uk) are one of the biggest retailers. There is also National Bee Supplies at Okehampton in Devon (www.beekeeping.co.uk) and there are several smaller companies as well.

Supers

Having just educated myself on the subject, I can now pass on to the reader the fact that supers are so named because that is the Latin for 'above' or 'over.' One super is not enough and you will need at least two or three per hive. The good news is that to construct a super, simply follow the same directions as for making a brood box. There is only one difference between a super and a brood box and that is the depth. The wood for the sides will therefore have to be cut to a slightly different prescription.

A super is three inches shallower than a brood box. It should measure 150mm or 5⅞" deep. Using 18mm ply, cut two pieces of ply to 460 x 150 mm. Cut another 2 plywood pieces to 424 x 132mm. These 4 pieces replace the equivalent pieces in the brood box instructions. The rest of the components and the methodology are precisely the same as for the brood box.

Crownboard

Cut a piece of ply to 46cm². Put a 7-9mm thick edging (up to 25mm wide) around the edge of one face of it. Make a mark in the middle of the board. Mark out an oval centred on your board that is 3 inches long with parallel sides set an inch apart. Essentially 3 holes of 25mm in diameter need to be drilled in a straight line so that they just all touch each other. A knife or saw can then be used to finish off a 3 inch long oval That's a simple crown board. The oval allows for the fitting of Porter bee escapes (a one way bee valve). The crownboard, when positioned over the brood box, can also be used as a clearance device to get bees out from the upper

A comparison of crown-
boards. Left - nucleus box,

honey supers.

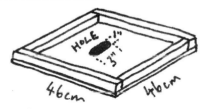

CROWN BOARD

Roof

As with any house, if the
roof isn't up to much, the
rest of the house will soon fall to pieces. The roof needs
to be covered in either metal sheeting or roofing felt. Even
a tidy job in polythene would work, although it might be
somewhat lacking in the beauty department.

Cut a piece of 18mm ply 520mm² (20½˝). Cut two sides
520 x 150mm (20½ x 6˝) and two further sides at 484 x
150mm (19⅛ x 6˝). You will also require some strips of
wood between 12 and 19mm (½ to ¾˝) thick and 19 -25mm
(¾ – 1˝) wide to hold the roof above the crown board.

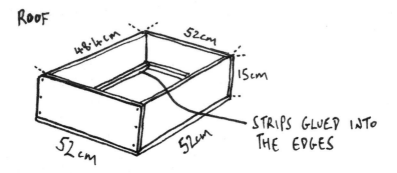

ROOF

48.4cm 52cm 15cm 52cm 52cm

STRIPS GLUED INTO THE EDGES

The roof can be assembled by forming the side pieces into a 520mm square using nails and glue. The top can be nailed and glued onto the sides. Turn the whole lot onto its top and glue some strips around the inside edges. This will strengthen the roof as well as keeping it raised up from the crownboard.

Finishing

Use sandpaper to finish off the joints on your hive and once again I shall reiterate the importance of sealing them from the weather with a suitable coating. Most wood treatments are poisonous to bees and will kill them so don't treat your hive on the inside. Coatings of varnish or paint should only be applied to the exterior. Leave the newly coated hive for a week or two before introducing your bees. Cuprinol clear comes in a green edged tin and, to my knowledge, it does not contain insecticides. I have used it with no problems.

When you get to siting your hive, either make yourself a simple wooden stand to keep it off the ground or use bricks or building blocks or whatever else you might have to hand. The flight path of bees from a hive can be controlled to an extent. This feature is particularly useful if keeping bees in a small area. They naturally want to fly at a height of about 10 feet (3metres) so if the hive is positioned with the entrance facing an obstacle, the bees will naturally fly upwards to overcome that object. Willow screening or old panel fencing can be used to separate the hive from the rest of the garden.

Avoid positioning beehives under trees if possible as it rains under trees long after the real rain has stopped. Shady areas under large trees can also reduce the hours per day of bee activity. If possible a hive should be sited out of a prevailing wind. Also avoid siting hives in cow fields unless you have electric fencing as hives make an attractive scratching target to cows. I've lost one myself to rampant bullocks! An open field or a small shady garden may be all you have to work with but the bees will generally survive and prosper wherever you site them. Do make sure you have sufficient working room around the hive as lifting supers full of honey can be a strenuous business.

A set of in-depth plans for the National hive were once issued as a government MAFF (Ministry of Agriculture, Food and Fisheries as it then was) document and can still be found on the internet in various places. If you fancy having a go at a proper woodworking project including the rebating and routing of timber, you can find more plans for a National hive at www.scottishbeekeepers.org.uk/learning/documents/nu mber%204%20national%20hive.pdf

Bee Feeders

In the autumn, if the bees have worked well and you have managed them well, you may be rewarded with a honey crop. After you have removed most of the honey from your beehives, you may have inadvertently left some of the colonies with insufficient stores to last them through the winter. Hives that are underweight in late September need to be offered a strong solution of sugar syrup in a feeder. Likewise, feed may also be needed to stimulate colony growth in the spring. Feeders are relatively easy to make. The overriding principle is to reduce the surface area of your

Build It!

A simple jar feeder is useful for delivering small quantities of sugar syrup to bees.

syrup offering to an acceptably small slot or hole so that the bees can't fall in and drown in it.

To fashion a quick bee feeder, simply take a clean 1lb honey jar with a screw top lid on it. Using a fine nail or a strong pin, puncture 10 or 12 fine holes in the centre. Fill the jar with syrup and invert it over the hole in the crown board. Plastic bucket feeders work on this principle but on a larger scale and they use a fine 35mm circular gauze in the lid. To make a feeder that will hold in excess of 5 litres you will need some more 18mm plywood. You will also need to use something along the lines of a silicon mold proof sealant to make the joints syrup tight. Cut the following plywood pieces:

2 top and bottom pieces of 400 x 214mm
2 long side pieces of 364 x 100mm
2 short side pieces of 214 x 100mm
2 pieces of 364 x 92mm

Using glue and nails, make a tray out of the side pieces and a bottom board. Take one of the pieces that measures 92mm width and fix it in position across the tray at a point about 10mm away from one of the long sides. This piece will contain the sugar syrup, the resulting 10mm slot will be dry. The inside of the syrup area could do with a coating of some sort eg. a carefully selected safe varnish. At any rate, all the joints will have to be sealed so that the sugar solution cannot leak out. A continuous bead of silicon sealant smeared into the joints works well. The final 92 x 364mm wooden

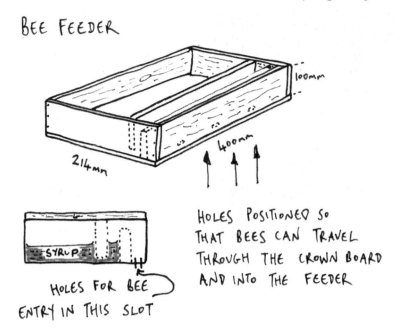

BEE FEEDER

100mm

214mm

400mm

SYRUP

HOLES FOR BEE
ENTRY IN THIS SLOT

HOLES POSITIONED SO
THAT BEES CAN TRAVEL
THROUGH THE CROWN BOARD
AND INTO THE FEEDER

piece should be positioned so that another 10mm slot is left between it and the previous one. The difference this time is that the final piece is mounted so that its top edge is flush with the top edges of the tray. It will leave a 0.8mm gap underneath it where the sugar syrup can flow.

The feeder top can be attached with a central screw in the middle of the feeding side of the tray. The lid can be slid over to one side to allow filling. The final job is to drill a series of bee holes along the bottom of the 10mm slot nearest to the side of the feeder. This will allow the bees through into the feeding space.

Bee Nucleus Box

During the warmer months of the year we can increase our colony numbers by making up nuclei of bees. Two strong brood frames full of bees nursing eggs and larvae, a component of flying bees and a frame of stores is the

Build It!

A home-made nucleus box. It's the internal dimensions that matter, not the external appearance.

minimum needed for a nucleus. Use at least 2 full frames of stores if it is late in the year and even then additional feeding may be required. These new starter colonies do not thrive particularly well if put into a full brood box so we use a nucleus box to get them 'going' and to keep them over the winter. A 'nuc' box is made to the same specifications as a brood box but is only wide enough to take five frames.

Remember that a brood box is 225mm or 8⅞″ deep. Using 18mm ply, cut two pieces of ply to 460 x 225 mm and another 2 pieces to 190 x 208mm.
You will also need:
2 x 190mm lengths of 25 x 38mm (1 x 1½″). (Approximate sizes would work equally well but one of the dimensions does need to be 25mm).
2 lengths of 12mm² or ½″² cut to 190mm.
2 more 190mm lengths of 38 x 12mm (1½″ x ½″)

In order to construct your 'nuc' box, follow the instructions as per the brood box, but where some of the brood box dimensions are given as 424mm, substitute this measurement with 190mm. The floor should be made up as per the brood box floor instructions but again, the overall width of the finished article needs only to be 225mm wide. A crown board of dimensions 460 x 225mm should be made to the same pre-scription as the larger crown board.

The roof doesn't need to be more than 2 or three inches deep. Use a piece of ply that's 280 x 420 and make up some ply sides that fix underneath it.

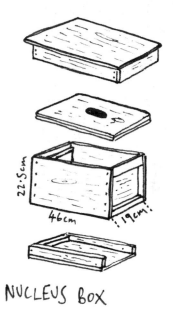

A NUC BOX IS ESSENTIALLY HALF A BROOD BOX

22.5cm

46cm

19cm

NUCLEUS BOX

Solar Wax Extractor

Hopefully you will get into beekeeping if you haven't already. I'd suggest that without management, the honey bee would be in peril in this country so more beekeepers are definitely needed. From time to time the beekeeper can end up with plenty of old bits of wax, blackened brood comb and general wax laden detritus. Of course it's a messy business rendering very valuable beeswax and I personally try and limit my waxy tribulations in the household kitchen to no more than once a year.

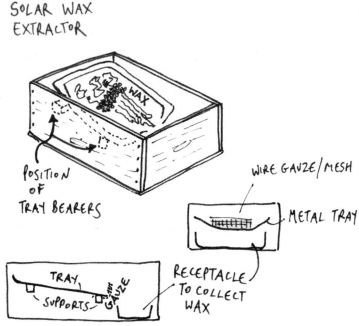

SOLAR WAX EXTRACTOR

POSITION OF TRAY BEARERS

WIRE GAUZE/MESH

METAL TRAY

TRAY SUPPORTS

RECEPTACLE TO COLLECT WAX

It's easy and inexpensive to build a solar wax extractor which will sort the beeswax from the dross and greatly reduce the amount of further processing required to obtain a finished product.

A solar wax extractor only works when the sun is shining with sufficient intensity and works on the same principle as solar hot water panels. The wax is placed in an insulated box behind a glazing panel. The inside of the cabinet is painted black and the whole arrangement is tilted at about 45 degrees towards the sun. Sufficient heat is thus generated for the wax placed at the high end of the box to melt and flow downward, leaving the muck and debris behind.

Construct the box to a size that relates to the number of hives you have. How much wax do you think you might need to render? If you have any pre-cut glass lying around, construct your project to suit that. Double glazing is best, but single glazing does work. I have built a working unit using a piece of perspex, although it wasn't as versatile as a glass paned extractor. You will need sufficient timber to make a box of the required size. As many of the projects thus far are given to making box like objects, I shall not go through the basics of making a box again. If in doubt please consult the chicken brooder section. For two or three hives, make an extractor that measures 40 x 60cm.

Use 12 or 18mm ply to make the cabinet and make it 25cm deep. At the bottom edge of the cabinet there must be a wax holding receptacle. If you go to the baking section of a discount shop (a pound shop or similar), you will find plenty of cheap metal-ware tins that will assist in this project. A small loaf tin or similar is ideal, although it might need bending a little.

The rest of the cabinet contains a metal shelf sloping down into the wax receptacle. A flat baking tray makes a good starting point here. You will need to bend the lower end of the tray so that the wax can flow off the bottom edge through a piece of fairly fine wire gauze. Mount the tray on lengths of batten screwed across the extractor. Wire gauze can be trapped between the lower support batten and the metal tray and bent upwards to interrupt the wax flow. By bending your cheap metal tray appropriately, you can funnel wax towards the centre.

GLASS FRAME

A simple frame is also needed to hold the glass pane. This can be made as follows:

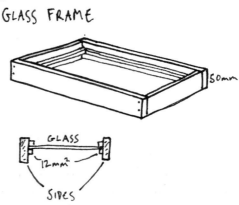

Use 50 x 25mm (2 x 1"). Make up a frame that will fit over the top of your extractor box. Use 2 pieces 610mm long and 2

Build It!

A small, perspex fronted solar wax extractor. Note how the detritus is left on the metal tray.

pieces 460mm long. Use 12mm² (½″²) wood to nail a rail around the inside of your frame that the glass will rest on. Fix the rail so that it is 12mm up from the bottom edge of the frame; this will leave sufficient frame depth for the glass and another round of 12mm beading to hold it in place.

The inside of the box can be improved by insulation if necessary, although I've never found it necessary. Paint the inside of the box black but don't bother to paint the metalwork as it will probably peel. On a warm day the box will get hot enough to cook in.............now there's an idea!

Honey Warming Cabinet

All honey granulates to a crystalline form, although the time taken to do this depends on both the original nectar source and the proliferation of granulation nuclei within the batch. The wider public has some great misconceptions about honey. A particularly emotive subject is that of oilseed rape honey, which quickly granulates into a very coarse, crystalline structure and, in my sales experience, seems to be particularly disliked by pensioners. What many people do not know, however, is that the structure of honey can be altered by a simple process known as seeding. By mixing at least five percent by volume of a smooth or soft textured honey into a fluid coarse variety, the resultant mix will eventually

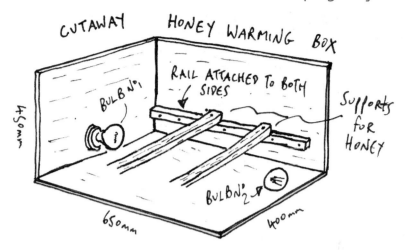

CUTAWAY   HONEY WARMING BOX

RAIL ATTACHED To BoTH SIDES

BULB N°1

450mm

Supports foR HoNEY

BULB N°2

650mm   400mm

granulate as a smooth soft set honey. It's very easy to alter the entire taste and texture of a coarse honey simply by seeding it and mixing it well. An electric drill with a whisk attachment makes a good and thorough mixing job.

To return honey from its crystalline state to a fluid, it needs to be warmed gently over a period of time. If you want to liquify one jar, simply stand it in some hot water but if you have a bucket of honey that needs melting, you will need a warming cabinet. If you want to make a large melting cabinet, find a redundant fridge, cut a 50mm hole at its top backside, find a surplus electric fan heater and cut a hole in the fridge to allow the hot air to be blown into the bottom of the compartment. Fill the fridge with honey and use the setup on a low heat setting. I've seen it done and it works well. If the fridge is holding the temperature well, set a timer to turn the heater on and off at intervals. Do use some common sense as regards any potential fire hazard. Some older fan heaters may possibly be prone to overheating.

To construct a small warming box which will accept a standard 30lb honey bucket you will need the following items, all made using 18mm ply:

Build It!

2 pieces 650 x 450mm - sides
2 pieces 364 x 450mm - ends
2 pieces 650 x 400mm – top and bottom

Insulation – polystyrene (poly tiles) or builders insulation.
Suitable screws nails and glue.

For the heat source you will also need:
2 x 5amp fused plugs
2m of flexible 240v cable
2 mains rated fixed light bulb holders (If one bulb goes out
you will still have the other one)
2 40w filament light bulbs

If you are not competent at wiring plugs and light bulbs,
then please find somebody to assist you who is. 240V
can kill! Construct the box as per the diagram and line it
with insulation. The box will need to function as an airing
cupboard so that the warmth is generated underneath the
honey buckets. Use 25 x 38mm to form a rail along the
inside of opposing sides of the cabinet. This rail will support
lengths of lath that will hold the honey buckets. The light
bulbs are situated at either end of the cabinet.

The bulb holders need to be safely wired to the cable and
two holes drilled in the cabinet ends through which the
cables can pass. The lamp holders can be screwed in place
inside the cabinet so that once the bulbs are in place, they
will be below the level of the slatted floor that the honey is
going to sit on. Plugs will obviously need wiring to the lamp
cables. The lid of the box could simply rest on the cabinet
or it could be hinged. It will, however, need some insulation
on its inside.

Last Gasp

Without proper trai-
ing and equipment,
beekeeping is not fun
and can be downright
dangerous. Before you
get any bees you will
need a suitable veil
that is 100% bee proof.
Other necessary at-
tire includes a zipped
boiler suit and wel-
lington boots. Leather
beekeeping gauntlets
are usually worn but
are losing favour due
to the possibility that
they harbor and help

Lighting a smoker is an acquired skill. A
blowlamp comes in handy.

spread bee diseases. Yellow marigold rubber gloves or sur-
gical gloves do not allow human scent to carry, can be dis-
infected between inspections and are often used as an alternative to gauntlets. A smoker is used to calm the bees both
before and during inspections. They are not costly and are
commonly used during bee manipulations in conjunction
with a hive tool.

Bees are best acquired from someone knowledgeable.
Expect to pay up to £90 for a healthy nucleus with a young
queen. The benefit of buying is that you will be getting a
quantity of known temperament. The problem with swarms
is that they are not always viable and can also be latent
carriers of bee diseases; they can also be extremely vicious.
Find someone in the know and you won't go far wrong. Set
out solely on your own and you may come to regret it.

Chapter Five
Using Plastic

Polytunnel

A north/south orientated dale, elevation 550ft, is not the sort of place that one is going to easily be able to germinate vegetables due to persistent late frosts. Although at this establishment, we do own a very tidy plastic green house, it is not noted for its aerodynamic qualities and in all probability it would soon get blown away if left erected all year round. The solution was to build a small 10ft x 15ft polythene greenhouse that would be both movable and resilient to the gale force winds that unpredictably sweep through the dale. Perhaps this is the solution for high and low altitude gardeners alike; a moderately sized and transportable greenhouse/animal shelter/bike shed on a shoestring.

Using materials to hand and a £40 order of horticultural polythene from a polytunnel manufacturer, the tunnel

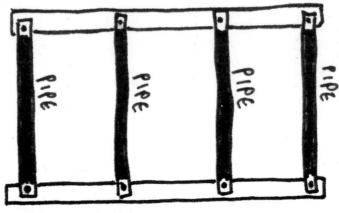

① FORM BASIC FRAME

greenhouse evolved with minor modifications over a period of a couple of days. Hoops were constructed from 25mm MDPE blue plastic water pipe, although in retrospect 32mm would have been a better choice. Four 5m lengths of pipe were drilled and screwed between two parallel 4.5m lengths of 3 x 2″ timber. One inch roofing batten was then bolted along the midpoint of all the plastic pipes. The theoretical width and height of the tunnel was worked out in accordance with the availability of standard polythene 'off the roll' sizes. As it was determined that 6m width was available, it was decided to make the external hoop measurement slightly under this.

Mathematically speaking the circumference of a circle = πd where pi = 3.14 (approx. constant) and d = the diameter of the circle; for a half circle we can use πr (radius).

So, using 5.5m width of polythene 5.5 = π r radius = 5.5/ 3.14 = 1.75m. So theoretically we could have a greenhouse 1.75m high and 3.5m wide. In reality, there is some latitude in sacrificing width for extra headroom during construction.

The whole affair was erected by bringing the 3 x 2″ timbers

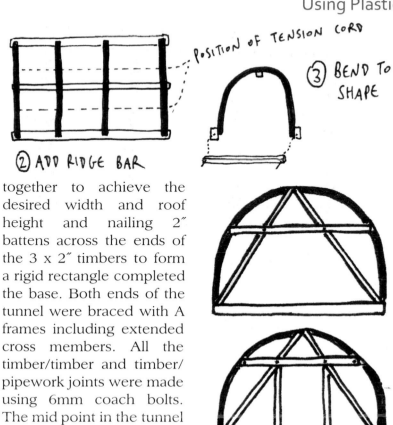

② ADD RIDGE BAR

POSITION OF TENSION CORD

③ BEND TO SHAPE

④ FORM ENDS

together to achieve the desired width and roof height and nailing 2″ battens across the ends of the 3 x 2″ timbers to form a rigid rectangle completed the base. Both ends of the tunnel were braced with A frames including extended cross members. All the timber/timber and timber/pipework joints were made using 6mm coach bolts. The mid point in the tunnel was also braced to the apex using an A frame of laths without a cross member.

Horticultural polythene is fixed directly to the base structure of the tunnel using battening and nails. It's a two man job putting on the skin and achieving a degree of tightness over the structure but it can be done so long as you don't expect to achieve a perfect finish as the design does have a degree of flexibility in it. The polythene passes underneath the base timber and is fastened on the inside of the greenhouse. The structure is anchored to the ground on the inside by four posts driven into the ground and nailed to the base structure. A door was made by first nailing in two upright lengths of batten

MAKE A LITTLE POLYTHENE COVERED DOOR

to create door posts. The door itself was a simple wooden frame with a cross bracing covered in polythene. The door is very light and is hung on 2 small steel hinges. Total cost? About £65.

The finished product didn't look too bad and was an instant success with Mrs J. An impromptu bench was constructed from brick piers and scaffold boards and in no time at all the monstrosity was filled with sprouting seedlings. An unexpected night of turbulence brought the addition of several fence posts driven into the ground along each side of the tunnel to which a mooring rope was tied. The tunnel is orientated the same way as the valley and to date it has withstood winds of over 50mph.

The greenhouse has celebrated its third anniversary so it certainly has been a cost effective project. Maintenance to date has included replacing lost bolts (the buffeting of the wind occasionally loosens and loses them) and minor fabric repairs. A modification incorporated at a later stage was the opening of a ventilation window in the top of the closed end. Quite simply, the structure was getting too hot on sunny days and required a through draft to ventilate it.

Cloches

These are not technically buildings, but it seems fit to add them after the polytunnel section as they are certainly of

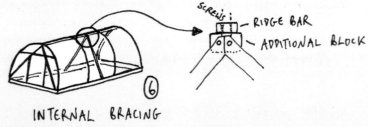

SCREWS
— RIDGE BAR
— ADDITIONAL BLOCK

INTERNAL BRACING

similar interest. Gardening in a bleak area, cloches are essential to keep seedlings safe from late frosts, but they also have a secondary motive; chicken prevention.

When seedlings are small, cut off demi-johns or clear plastic pots can suffice for protection but when it comes to buying several metres of cloche, things can start getting a little expensive. Offcuts from a polytunnel or even a small order of horticultural polythene can be used to construct modestly priced cloches. First decide how wide and how high you wish your cloche to be and work out the width of polythene accordingly. The hoops are another matter. For a small cloche just 20cm high, coat hanger wire made into hoops every 40cm would suffice. As the wire is thin, it would need to be attached to something with a greater diameter (eg. pegs of wood) that can be pushed into the soil and remain upright. For a larger cloche, offcuts of 15mm flexible plastic piping can be used to form hoops that can be pushed straight into the ground. If you don't have anything suitable to form hoops, make a triangular (or square) frame out of garden twine and canes and cover that with polythene. To fasten the polythene to the frame or hoops, use carpet or duct tape which has excellent adhesive properties as long as it's applied to a dry surface.

Clear Corrugated Plastic

It's possible to make cloches out of clear lengths of corrugated plastic. Add a piece of wooden batten down each side of the length of plastic using screws and washers and bend the plastic over to form a tunnel shape. By banging four pegs into the ground corresponding to the width and length of your plastic tunnel, you will be able to wedge the bent over sheet in between the pegs and screw the bottom edge to the wooden pegs.

Polycarbonate sheeting is now used for greenhouses as well as conservatory roofs. It doesn't last forever but long after it has come off a roof, it can be put to other uses. Cut two pieces to size and, using duct tape, adhere the lengths together with a long flexible tape hinge. Position the plastic tent over your plants and, if necessary, fasten it to the ground with some pegs.

Ideas for Plastic Bottles

The powers that be reckon that in 50 years time it may be economically viable to mine current landfill sites for the plastics they contain. It really is a shame that so much of our plastic gets buried. Where possible I like to make use of the local council's efforts to collect recyclable materials, but unfortunately our local scheme doesn't cover plastics, which are probably the second biggest waste product after paper.

Over the past few years I have developed a number of uses for plastic packaging and other by-products which would otherwise have simply been thrown away. These uses have ranged from the sublime to the ridiculous, but do illustrate what one can achieve with a little imagination. I have tried various ideas to give bottles a slightly longer life before they go into the bin. Admittedly they don't last particularly long but then again, most of us do have a steady supply. The Robinson's brand in particular are made of a particularly durable plastic and have lent themselves to various uses around the garden and beyond. Some of the larger plastic bottles have a moulded handle and, when cut off approximately 3 inches below the handle, make very good feed scoops. When taking poultry to market it seems only fair that they should have a drink whilst in those horrible little auction cages. I've seen various manipulations of 1 litre milk cartons providing water for birds. The simplest is just the bottom 2 inches of a bottle, steadied with a few choice stones in it. A more complicated drinker can be formed by cutting a sizable rectangle out of the front of a plastic milk bottle; the hole is big enough so that the bird can drink from water in the bottom of the bottle. By making a cut in the plastic handle, a sort of hook can be created by which to secure the bottle to the side of the poultry cage. One litre and 500ml bottles laid flat with a few decent circular holes cut out of a side also make excellent feeders for chick crumbs and are ideal for newly hatched birds.

A plastic bottle as a feeder, holes are cut to let the feed out.

The one and two litre bottle sizes, if cut in half at the correct point, also produce free pots to germinate seeds in. The tapering end of a bottle can be used as a small cloche to offer seedlings protection after planting out. The deep plastic trays in which the supermarkets sell their mushrooms make excellent germinating trays. A piece of cling film over the top and a warm window ledge is all that's needed to get some seeds going. By far the best use I have made of a plastic bottle so far is as a chicken feeder. Holes were cut around the base of a 3 litre squash bottle and the base of this bottle was then screwed to a shallow dish. The feeder is filled through the top using another half bottle as a feed scoop and funnel. The whole affair is suspended from a tripod of garden canes to keep it clear of rats. But a chicken feeder only costs £5 I hear you wail!

Build It!

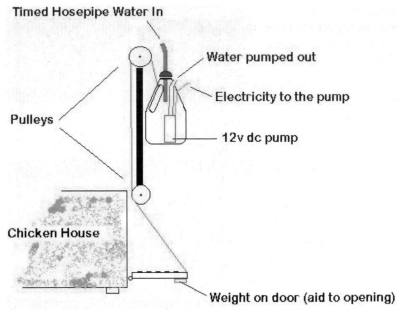

Timed Hosepipe Water In

Water pumped out

Electricity to the pump

Pulleys

12v dc pump

Chicken House

Weight on door (aid to opening)

Heath Robinson Automatic Door System

A 3 litre squash bottle was used in the construction of a slightly 'Heath Robinson' affair for opening and closing the chicken house door at night. I shall endeavour to explain the construction, known locally as 'Auto Chicken.'

The system relies on a timed greenhouse watering system. The timer, of the type made by Hozelock, I believe, fits directly to an outside tap and is able to be adjusted to deliver anywhere between 1 minute and 1 hour of water at a given time of day. By setting the device to deliver 1 minute of water at dusk, a large plastic bottle is filled via the hosepipe which in turn acts as a counterbalance weight to the chicken house door (see diagram). In the mornings, a small 12-volt electric pump switches on for a minute at a pre-determined time, thereby emptying the water out of the bottle and resulting in the opening of the door. The pump is operated using a shop bought digital timer of the type used to switch household lights on or off whilst on holiday. An old mains to 12 volt

Scalextrix transformer is plugged into the timer in the garage to provide the power for the 12 volt electric pump. The pump used, in this instance, is a fairly powerful Whale pump, although a better bet would probably be a cheap or redundant windscreen washer pump from a car, which, although less powerful, could simply be switched on for slightly longer to empty the water weight.

Heath Robinson style door opener. The hose lets water in, the pump (inside the bottle) pumps the water out again

The system has had minor problems; it doesn't allow for variations in day length and the timers do need tweaking every 2 or 3 weeks in the summer. It is a great boon though, especially if I need to go away for a night or two. I reckon as a future modification I'd go for a two pump closed circuit system where water is simply pumped to the high bottle at night and down again in the morning. This arrangement can be built from junk or spares and can be made on a far lower budget than any commercially available door opening system.

Build It!

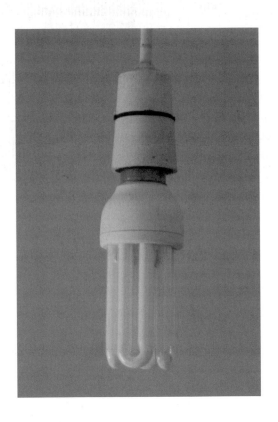

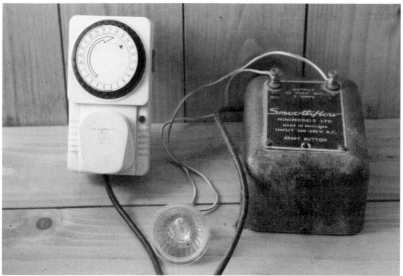
The essential elements of a timed hen house lighting system.

Chapter Six
Electrical Projects

Electric Fencing

There's nothing better for making quick field enclosures than electric fencing. It works on nearly all livestock, although that said, sheep are troublesome to keep in. Fences can be constructed either by fixing commercially available plastic insulators to existing wooden fence posts or by running electric tape or wire through cheap plastic electric fencing stakes. Wire is best for farm animals but electric tape is preferred for horses as they are not renowned for their visual acuity and may not see wire.

All electric fencing units have a specific energy output that governs the total amount of cable or netting that they can power. Fencing units emit a high voltage low current pulse into the fence line. When something, for example a cow, touches the fence, an electrical circuit is completed and a pulse of electricity earths itself through the animal to the ground, hence delivering a small shock. If the fencing system is earthed prematurely, either by plants or undergrowth, electrical leakage occurs and the efficacy of the fence is reduced. This does not mean to say in all instances that the fence will not work. My electric poultry fences are probably sagging on the floor and earthing out in several places but I have tested them and know that they still work because I am only running 100m of fencing from a reasonably powerful fencing unit. When I was a kid, we used to test whether fences were switched on by holding a blade of green grass against the fence. This offered an electrical resistance and meant that you only got a tingling sensation in your fingers rather than a cow sized belt. For less than a fiver one can buy a small device (a lamp with an earthing wire) that will test your fence without the need for self imposed torture. My personal preference is for battery fencing units as they are portable and allow me to fence against livestock damaging my beehives; batteries do run flat, however! 240v fencers are useful; they don't run flat and can be kept permanently connected to the mains in an out-building from where the output can be safely 'piped' around the farm using purpose designed insulated cable. If you try to use normal insulated cable to carry electric fence voltages it will work....but only for a while. The high voltages (8-12 000 volts) will eventually break down the cable insulation which was only designed to cope with an intended voltage of 240v. You will then get earthing from the 'insulated' wire.

Hen House Lighting Projects

During the winter months hens will often go off laying due to decreasing daylight hours. An easy way to remedy this problem and thus maintain a steady supply of fresh eggs throughout the winter is to give the hens artificial light in their houses. There are many different ways of skinning the proverbial cat and not all of them will suit you.

Mains Powered Lighting

Once again, don't mess with 240v unless you are sure what you are doing. Ensure that all lights and cables are appropriately isolated when working on them and, if cable runs extend outdoors, ensure you have an adequate residual current device (RCD) in the line. Mains powered lighting is only suitable for large poultry houses where the bulbs and cables are out of both damp conditions and harm's way. At the simplest level, a commercially available working lamp of any type could be hung up in a poultry shed and powered with a decent extension lead. The addition of a cheap electrical timer at the indoor end will provide a method of automatic switching on and off. Energy saving bulbs should be used if possible.

12v and Battery Powered Lighting

For those of us with smaller hen houses, 12 volt lighting systems are the way forward as they are, in relative terms, electrically safe. Use 12 volt automotive light bulbs and lamp holders which may be found at any car accessory shop. Alternatively, you could use 12v halogen down lighter bulbs but they are more expensive and power hungry.

The power supply can be from either a 240/12v dc adapter, a charged car battery or a battery charger located in a shed. For low power applications such as this, the cable need only be inexpensive 2 core door bell wire or something similar. The advantage of using a 240v power supply transformer and running 12volts out to your hen house is that you can plug the transformer into a timer unit. If running power to several small hen houses, wire the light bulbs in parallel across the power supply cable. In the event of one bulb blowing, the others will all remain on.

Halogen bulbs can be bought separately or in a kit with their own power transformer. Unfortunately, these transformers won't supply sufficient current to power the bulbs if the length of cable between them and the bulb exceeds 2 metres. This can be resolved by buying a waterproof transformer which can live outdoors, hence using a short 12v cable run into the hen house. It doesn't, however, alleviate the problem of live 240 volt cables around the place. If using halogen bulbs, wire them on a 12 volt cable run from a suitable 12v power source such as a car battery charger.

Recent innovations in LED lighting are probably the low power future of many lighting applications. Generally, the collection of LED torches I possess all take 3 batteries requiring between 3.6 and 4.5 volts to power them. I have been bequeathed a set of stick on 'press to illuminate' button LED lights which can be positioned almost anywhere. These items again require 3 batteries each to power them; by wiring 3 of these units in series, they could be made to run from any 12 volt supply at very low current.

12 Volt Incubator

All incubators have one fundamental flaw and that is that in the event of a power cut you will probably lose the lot. So far it's happened to me twice but on one of those occasions I was very quick with the petrol generator, thus saving the eggs. With a 12 volt incubator, you can simply rig it up to a car battery.

Temperature control is the fundamental basis of any incubator and, whilst it is fair to say that the other ingredient is correct humidity, the second cannot be obtained without the first. Chicken eggs generally incubate over a 21 day period and require a steady temperature of 37.5°C (100°F). Traditional incubators often worked on some sort of partially evacuated capsule that would expand and contract as the temperature in the incubator altered; this in turn altered a mechanical linkage, thus controlling the heat source. Modern incubators rely on electronic temperature control and nowadays employ an electric heat source instead of a paraffin heater. A hen naturally turns and tends her eggs during the sitting period and, in some incubators, this process is replicated by electro mechanical gently see-sawing egg trays. Basic incubators don't possess egg turners and so, as the overseer, one acquires the laborious task of daily turning of the eggs by hand.

A polystyrene box suitable for making an incubator.

Temperature control in this unit comes courtesy of a commercially available thermostat kit, available from the electronics company Maplin for about five pounds. These units are manufactured by Velleman and were recommended to me by my father who is an electronics engineer and semi-retired college lecturer. Having searched around extensively, most air sensing thermostat units do not operate in the 30 – 40°C range and are therefore unsuitable for egg incubation. The Velleman unit has actually been designed to allow modification of the temperature range by the substitution of one component

A Velleman thermostat. It comes as a kit and does require soldering together.

at a cost of a few extra pence. There are additional similar electronic thermostat kits by other manufacturers that would work equally well. There are also plenty of commercially available incubator kits and projects and all the designs are fairly similar so there's nothing new, just a variation on a theme.

This is a 12 volt project and finding budget low power heat sources can be particularly troublesome. Low power heat

Build It!

filaments can be wound from resistance wire but these do not last very long. As the relay in this circuit will only switch up to a maximum of 70 watts, we are fairly limited in our choices of heat source. With regards once again to my dad, who ran some experiments on potential low power heat sources, the best option does seem to be quartz halogen down lighter bulbs. Why these bulbs seem so popular beats me. They are incredibly inefficient and produce far too much heat for the amount of light they create. Two 25 watt bulbs wired in parallel through the thermostat relay, make a simple heater unit. By having two bulbs, an element of safety is built in to the design; if one bulb fails you won't loose all the developing chicks.

The incubator does need insulating to reduce heat loss. Kingspan (building insulation) or polystyrene is ideal for this. Your incubator doesn't really want to be larger than 30 x 30cm internally and between 15 and 20cm deep. All sides, top and bottom need insulation. The top and bottom also need three or four ventilation holes 5mm in diameter. Temperature monitoring is important and can only be done successfully with a thermometer inside the incubator. A

small plastic window in the lid about 5 x 10cm allows one to see inside, and if a small thermometer is left in the incubator it can easily be read.

This container had previously been an incubator. The device had irretrievably packed up and was an ideal insulated candidate.

Before the all important diagrams I'll discuss the use of a fan. There are two types of incubator; forced air and still air. I have converted a still air model and found that the hatch rate improved with a small internal fan. Cheap 12 volt computer fans are ideal for this application and allow a more even spread of warm air throughout the incubator. An incubator will, however, still work without this addition.

If you build one of these incubators and have some fertile eggs, take note of the following practical incubation points :

Perfect, after some adjustment. The temperature holds steady.

- Eggs are fertile for up to 3 weeks after they have been laid, but 2 – 14 days is best.
- Wash the eggs in an egg disinfectant before incubation for optimum results.
- The eggs should have been left indoors to acclimatise to room temperature before use.
- The incubator should not be positioned in areas of variable temperature eg. windowsills.
- The incubator should be run up and adjusted correctly before introducing any eggs.
- The eggs need turning daily, gently and quickly so the overall temperature doesn't reduce.
- Candle the eggs at seven days and discard any that are not fertile.
- At day 19 introduce a water tray into the incubator and maintain its contents. Close off the top ventilation holes so the water evaporates and increases the humidity for hatching.

Manipulation of the Thermostat Kit

The thermostat kit needs to be soldered together as per the instructions included in it. Referring to the printed circuit board you will see that the position marked R5 (resistor) is also marked R5↓ Tmax↑. This means that if R5, which is rated at 120kΩ, is reduced in value then the maximum operating temperature of the thermostat will be increased.

Build It!

Inside of the working incubator showing the heat source, fan and heat sensing thermistor.

The 2 options available to us are either to adjust the value of R5 from 120k to 94k (2 x 47k wired in series) or alternatively to adjust the sensing thermistor from 10k to 15k. The thermistor will need to be attached to 30cm of wire so that it can be positioned inside the incubator whilst the electronics stay outside.

Construction of the Incubator

Either insulate a container you already have or make a small plywood box and line it with polystyrene. The lamps need to be mounted so that they are completely inside the box, but not in such a position that they can cook any of the eggs. To this end, mount the lamps near the top of the incubator. A strip of wood across the box will give something to support them. If using a fan, attach it to one side of the box with either tape or self-tapping screws.

Incubator Wiring Diagram

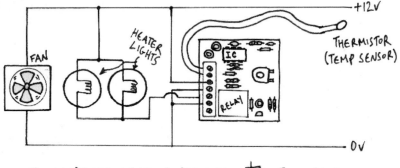

THE LAMPS ARE WIRED IN PARALLEL. If ONE BLOWS, THE OTHER WILL STAY ON.
IF THE LAMPS WERE WIRED IN SERIES THEY WOULD BE WIRED LIKE THIS :

Quick Egg Candling

Traditional candling of eggs was done in a darkened room in front of... yes you've guessed it, a candle. Times may have moved on but squinting at an egg in front of a bright light in a dark room still remains the favoured way of checking fertility and embryo development. Cut a piece of board so that it's big enough to sit over the lens of a bright halogen torch or will completely block the light from a metal desk lamp. Drill a hole the size of a 5 pence piece in the middle of your board. The egg will be candled by placing it over this narrow light source. Either carefully juggle the whole affair or tape the board in place. What you are looking for is a system of blood vessels emerging from the developing embryo. I can say little more in this book. Discard any eggs you are certain are infertile. They tend to break, crack, explode or generally make a stinking nuisance of themselves later on.

A private moorland water supply reservoir. The source is up close to the very distant rocky edge in the top right of the photo. This tank will go for several months through dry periods.

Chapter Seven
Water, Water Everywhere

We take water for granted. On goes the tap, out comes the water. We have water restrictions when the oceans are full of it and we have damaging flash flooding when reservoirs and supplies are seemingly low. For the benefit of water on tap and our sewage floating merrily away, we pay money.... in fact quite a lot of money. Most people haven't got much idea how much they pay to the water companies and neither have I because, thankfully, I don't have to pay.

For a smallholder, water conservation is of paramount importance; water for crops, water for beasts and water for the house. It's all too easy to say, "Well, I'm not on a meter," but I can assure you that one day you will be. Having once worked for a brief spell with a water company, I can confidently state that clean water is fast becoming a costly commodity. When a third or more of supplies are lost underground prior to reaching the consumer and pipe networks are in constant need of updating, somebody has to foot the bill. To quote the lottery "It could be you!"

And it's not just the supply network that is stretched. Thousands of acres of concrete, tarmac and roof tiling are added to the UK's infrastructure every year; millions of gallons of water that would have otherwise soaked away into the ground are redirected through culverts, drains and sewers into watercourses that cannot bear the burden. Your water bill is actually divided into two parts; a water segment and a sewerage segment. There are a multitude of measures that every householder (flats largely excused) in the UK could and should take to cut down on water consumption and usage, from economical toilet cisterns to taking showers instead of baths. In the main we shall look at how water supplies can be both harvested and preserved in an agriculturally useful way.

Water Butts and Automatic Plant Watering

At the simplest level, free water can be harvested using a water butt. Some of the larger containers will hold close to 500 litres. A short internet search will reveal 1000 litre plastic steel caged industrial containers for less than £50. That's quite a lot of water! Commercially available rainwater harvesting kits can also now be purchased, although I'd strongly suggest that anyone with even the faintest grasp of plumbing could make their own using the wide array of plastic and push fit plumbing systems now available. Simply speaking a length of guttering on a house, shed or greenhouse roof will serve as the source collection point. Investing in one of those in-line (downpipe fitted) rain savers (they're about £5) is handy as it sends the water onwards back into the drain should the water butt become full. Unless you want your water full of bloodworm and jokers (as fishermen refer to them) during the warmer months, you'll find it necessary to seal the container to prevent entry to mosquitoes and suchlike that produce these larvae. Probably the most industrious use of a small water butt is to drip feed or automatically water one's greenhouse full of plants and seedlings. Hoselock produce timed water valves that will control the flow to your plants as and when you want it. Admittedly, the initial outlay might be high, but the equipment will last for years, it conserves water and, once set up, it doesn't half save time spent watering.

Utilising Natural Water Sources

At this point I'm not suggesting that everyone disconnect their houses from the supply network. My own situation is unique in that mains water and sewage are not available and, even if they ever were, surely the local farms would revolt against their planned introduction. Pipework and delivery aside, there are essentially four elements to any small scale water supply chain for domestic or agricultural use. These are: a) Source b) Storage c) Filtration d) Point of use.

The source in my example is a stream running over the moor edge some 500m distant and 500ft higher up the valley. This source is disadvantageous in that it is open and could be subject to contamination from flies, faeces, dead sheep....etc etc, so let's not even go there. At the source is a primary collection chamber (plastic, 25 litres) filled with gravel which acts as a rough filter to remove large debris. This primary collection point is piped to a secondary plastic water tank where the outflow pipe towards the house is mounted 6 inches up from the bottom of the tank. A shut off tap is mounted on the outside of this small settling tank. A degree of protection from sediment and detritus ingestion is afforded by having the delivery pipe mounted 15cm higher than the tank bottom. The water flows downhill through a 25mm blue MDPE plastic pipe buried underground. 100m distant from my house and perhaps 70 ft higher in elevation

Build It!

is the water storage facility. This is a purpose built 5000 litre black plastic tank set into the side of the hill. Normally this quantity of water would be mounted on a concrete base but as we are on hard shale, an insulating/surface smoothing layer of Kingspan sufficed as a base. Inside the tank the inflow pipe terminates in a gigantic ball valve. This has the disadvantage that when the ball valve is closed, the pressure in the uphill side of the pipe can build up to 10 bar (147psi) with the backed up water. A future option is to fit an overflow into the tank, discharging the run-off through a pipe to a distant watercourse. Unfortunately the continuous flow of this system is very low so it can't be used as a renewable energy source.

From the storage tank a pipe runs directly to the house with tap off points for outside usage. Inside the property there is no cold water storage tank, only a header tank for hot water. In effect, the body of stored water up the hill maintains mains pressure.

Filtration for drinking water was initially provided by a reverse osmosis water treatment plant and use of 3rd taps. All other domestic water supply is direct, unfiltered from the distant storage tank. All the properties in this locality are the same, yet there is no record of illness through water contamination. Inside the house is a water meter which was needed before deregulation of water abstraction (light private users) by the Environment Agency. The continued use of the meter is handy as I can work out both average usage and also know if a minor internal leak occurs. As it currently stands, we are using between 2.5 – 3 cubic metres of water a month which, in theory, also gives us a reserve of 6 – 8 weeks in the storage tanks should a drought occur!

The stated reverse osmosis filtration system packed up within a short period of use due to the high levels of minerals, peat and fine sediment within the water. Under examination the 5 stage filter system was quickly becoming clocked up, requiring frequent changes of all components. Regular filter changes are feasible but are a costly option, so an alternative was sought.

This sort of set-up could be adapted for several different water sources. The problem in most cases will be insufficient head of water to provide a usable water pressure. In situations where water is available but with no head the following methods are an option:

Direct pumping as needed – electric, manual or wind driven.
Electric pumping on reduced night electricity tariffs to a storage vessel.
Electric pumping using renewable energy (wind or solar) to a storage vessel.
Use of a 'ram' where water flow is available (i.e. using a progressive water weight to raise a small amount of water in height).
Boreholes are one way of exploiting a free water supply in some areas, although the cost of sinking one would more than likely prove prohibitive for a light user.

Water Filtration and Purification

There are various methods available to filter spring water, thus rendering it fit for consumption. If you've got time to make activated charcoal, then that's about the best there is for a filter bed. Generally speaking I am only concerned about removing biological pathogens from my drinking water supply, cryptosporidium and suchlike. I do know that my water supply contains high levels of iron, although I do read my wife's British Medical Journal on a regular basis and haven't found this to be a major cause for concern. You can get your water tested but that can lead to a whole host of problems if the testing authority condemns your supply. An acquaintance fell foul of such procedure and was issued with a notice of intended prosecution should he fail to get

Build It!

his supply up to standard. He was forced to buy x, y and z from a, b or c, with no other options allowed, and at a costly sum. None of his neighbours, incidentally, ever went down the same testing avenue.

Water filtration units are available at low cost, although what they filter out is both variable and debatable. A filter of less than 5 microns is required to remove most biological hazards. Pre-filters are required simply to avoid clogging the fine filters with larger particles. The water bills inevitably come in the shape of replacement cartridges, although a three year supply for 50 quid isn't really too bad. The best method of killing biological nasties is to run your water through a pre-filter to take out the bits and then run it through an ultra violet (UV) treatment unit. When pathogens are subjected to intense UV light in such a unit, the light breaks down the RNA, thus killing the cells. Interestingly enough, a team of researchers recently discovered that simply leaving contaminated water in a plastic bottle in the sun killed off most of the bugs (somewhere in excess of 90% I believe). This was billed as a breakthrough method of simple purification for developing countries. Household UV water treatment systems are costly to buy and undeservedly so. Allegedly the cheap UV filtration systems required for tropical fish are not up to the standard required for human consumption. Here's the author's version of events.

I purchased a very nice £500 water purifier via eBay for a meagre £125 or so. Essentially, it consists of a pre-filter, followed by a water jacket around a glass tube in which a UV light is situated. On examination of the unit, the UV tube was found to be manufactured by Tropical Marine (obviously for aquarium purposes). I made enquiries with various spares companies and found that the numerical code on the 15 watt tube was correct for this unit. Therefore there does not appear to be any apparent difference in the light output of a household unit compared to a much cheaper tropical fish unit. There is, however, a correlation between

DIY WATER SUPPLY

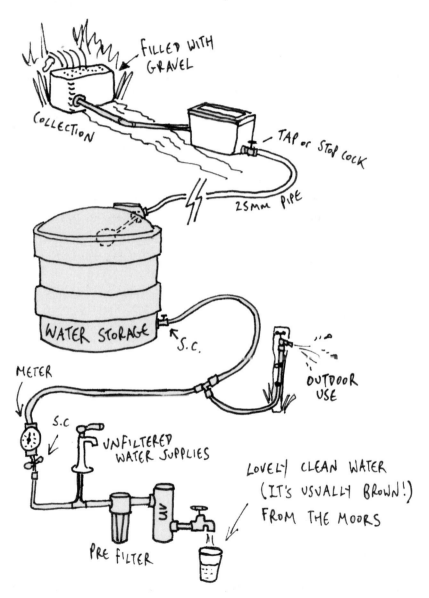

FILLED WITH GRAVEL

COLLECTION

TAP or STOP COCK

25MM PIPE

WATER STORAGE

S.C.

METER

S.C

OUTDOOR USE

UNFILTERED WATER SUPPLIES

PRE FILTER

UV

LOVELY CLEAN WATER
(IT'S USUALLY BROWN!)
FROM THE MOORS

the UV tube's electrical rating and the maximum amount of water (litres/minute) that can be safely passed through the light chamber for effective sterilisation. The aquarium units have not been certified for household use and therefore the manufacturers charge their true worth, not an inflated price. I do have a posh certified unit but I am adamant that I would drink water that had been filtered and passed through a similar aquarium set up. Over time, UV tubes do lose their intensity and they must be replaced on a periodically. In my case it's every 12 months.

Sewage

Sewerage and grey water disposal is a problem that was solved for the masses by the invention of the flush toilet (sorry to spoil the myth but Thomas Crapper didn't invent it). Sewers might have helped to clean up our industrialised cities but they did nothing for our rivers, wildlife or polluted coastal seas. The addition to water of waste bodily products is not the best or most efficient way of disposing of said material. Unfortunately it is generally the only solution that present economics will permit. Broadly speaking, aside from mains networks, these are the other methods that are recognised ways of sewage disposal: cess pit, septic tank, reed bed, biodisc or other commercially developed means and self-composting toilets.

In reality, the first method is not a method of disposal but a temporary holding measure that requires regular emptying. Many folk will anecdotally tell you that septic tanks do not need emptying, but this is nonsense. Septic tanks work by allowing solid material to settle out and break down under anaerobic bacterial action. Grey water runs off into a system of underground pipework where it gradually drains away. Tanks can run for very many years without emptying, all the time gently silting up the pipework that drains the system and eventually they will cease to work. Bespoke reed beds are now recognised and approved by building regulations as a method of cleaning up waste water prior to discharge. The reeds absorb nutrients from the effluent which is percolated through a system of planted beds. These systems are useful in conjunction with septic tanks where drainage and run off are a problem. An alternative method for use in areas where there is no alternative but to discharge effluent is a biodisc plant marketed by Titan. This does require yearly emptying but relies on electrics, bacterial and mechanical wizardry to ensure that the effluent discharge is nigh on drinkable.

The one true method of sewage disposal that is environmentally friendly is the self-composting toilet. I shall not go into a lengthy description of the 2 compartment yearly changed outside privy but rather the high tech end of what this has become. Type "self-composting toilet" into eBay on a global search and you will see what I mean. The modern toilet, as manufactured by Envirolet, requires no water whatsoever. These stand alone units require limited power and a stench pipe. The toilet works by using low powered heat to evaporate off excess moisture from the loo. The addition of a little magic ingredient and regular manual rotation of the waste drum (via an external cranking handle) ensures rapid and even composting. Open a drawer at the bottom of the bog on a monthly basis and a crumbly brown compost can be removed and spread on your artichokes if you feel so inclined. The cost for all this by the time you've paid import tax and whatnot is probably a shade under £1000. The problem with all this is that, to my knowledge, the building authorities are still reluctant to embrace such technology, i.e. your costly new throne will still not manage to absolve you of your sewerage charges; you simply can't get your house disconnected. If you could, the thousand pound potty might well pay for itself in 4 years providing it ran maintenance free and you installed a filter to clean up the rest of your household grey water prior to discharge (comparatively easy). If I ever find myself with a spare pound or more, I may well invest in one of these contraptions, or even better, I may try my hand at building one myself (see chapter 9 for thoughts on this issue). Water conservation isn't necessarily about implementing lots of silly ideas, it's about making the best and most economical use of what you have. A car doesn't need paid for chloro-fluorinated water to clean it and neither do plants. My late Grandma's aspidistra once thrived on cold tea!

Although some of these ideas may be out of reach for your dwelling, the addition of a simple water butt, drip fed into a chicken drinker or suchlike, will help to reduce your overall water consumption. John Seymour once said, concerning his toilet: "If it's yellow let it mellow, if it's brown flush it down." Water preservation indeed.

Simple Septic Tank

This is a useful method of creating a drain system with a soak away for an outside loo or an occasionally used guest quarters such as a caravan. It comprises of a series of plastic barrels that act as solid traps and allow the grey water to flow away. Systems such as this use bacteria to break down the solids and are easily spoiled by the addition of strong soaps, chemicals or bleach. Like any septic tank, the sediment barrels will need emptying occasionally, On a small unit like this with occasional use, it may take a year or two before it ever needs maintenance, then it's simply an exercise of moving buckets of digested slosh to a compost heap. Mmmm, you can even use it to grow veg if you have the stomach for it.

You will need two industrial 120 litre plastic barrels with lids. These are used in the food and chemical industries and can be found on the internet for a small sum of money. The bins need connecting with 2 through tank connectors and 30cm or so of plastic waste pipe. Use plastic 32 or 40mm push fit waste fittings. Connect the two tanks at about the same level, 15cm down from the top. In one of the tanks you will need an inlet for a waste pipe and in the other you will need

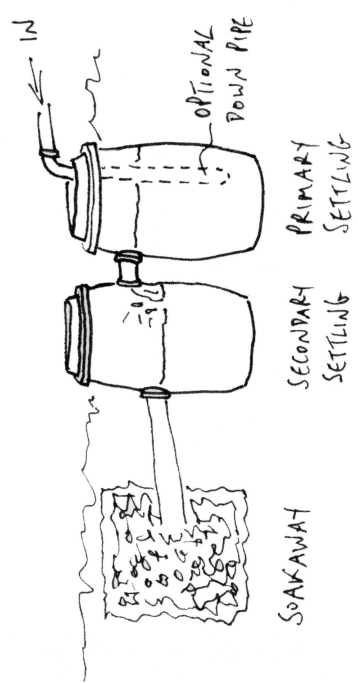

SIMPLE SEPTIC TANK

IN

OPTIONAL DOWN PIPE

PRIMARY SETTLING

SECONDARY SETTLING

SOAKAWAY

an outlet pipe about 30cm down the side. Dig a hole in the ground and sit the bins in the hole, ensuring the connecting pipe is either level or slightly downhill from entry to exit tank. The hole can also be used as a soakaway if the ground is reasonably well drained. Backfill the holes with gravel, leaving the tops of the tanks visible. If you have heavy soil or clay, you may need to make a better soakaway. Either use a gravel filled trench with a percolated pipe embedded in it (you can percolate any pipe yourself by cutting slots with an angle grinder) or alternatively dig a hole that will take a cubic yard of gravel and pipe the run off into that. I have used both techniques with satisfactory results.

Thoughts on Self-Composting Toilets

Self composting toilets are not a new thing, but with dwindling water resources they may yet again come into their own. The outdoor 2 compartment loo might do for the permanently outdoors or the temporarily insane but it is doubtful that they will catch on in the average modern semi. There are, however, modern space age self-composting thrones that can be fitted indoors and render all that is due them into a dry, brown, crumbly mixture. Such toilets are not cheap and can be seen on the internet manufactured by companies such as Envirolet and Sun-Mar.

I would like to find the time to build and trial one of these units as I have an extremely good idea of how they work. I will endeavor to explain the basic toilet architecture and then, if any hapless reader feels brave enough to take it on, you can let me know how the finished item works. Please don't send samples.

Essentially, inside the toilet is a small rotary composter that does require the occasional addition of sawdust, peat or suchlike. This part of the device could be made from a small plastic or stainless steel litter bin. The toilet needs to have a stench pipe that is plumbed to the outside. By putting a

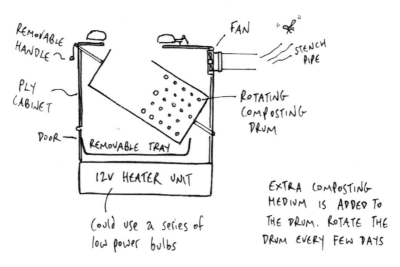

PROTOTYPE SELF COMPOSTING TOILET

REMOVABLE HANDLE

FAN "❋"

STENCH PIPE

PLY CABINET

ROTATING COMPOSTING DRUM

DOOR

REMOVABLE TRAY

12V HEATER UNIT

Could use a series of low power bulbs

EXTRA COMPOSTING MEDIUM IS ADDED TO THE DRUM. ROTATE THE DRUM EVERY FEW DAYS

small electric fan inside the cabinet, air is forced out through the pipe and an airflow through the toilet cabinet is created. This has two effects; firstly it prevents external odour around the toilet and secondly it aids drying of the compost and unmentionable liquids contained in the device.

The toilet also requires a small heat source to aid evaporation of liquid. Underneath the composter there should be a collection tray and underneath that would be a heat source. I suspect you won't be trying it. Have a look at the outline diagram. It genuinely is a good idea and could be achieved with a little trial and error.

Drainage

Having suggested methods of extracting water from watercourses, it's worth pointing out what to do if you have too much of the stuff and it's lying all over your land. It's not rare that I have something to do with other people's drains as I have a little mini-digger which is at times very much in demand. There are good drainage jobs and very poor ones. The poor ones don't bother to cover the drain with a layer of stone and will pack up in no time at all.

Drainage pipe comes in flexible, perforated lengths in diameters varying from 50mm (2″) upwards. It is effective in allowing water to seep into it and provides a clear channel for that water to pass through. Most fields have had drainage work done to them at one time or another but maintenance is a different issue. Clay field drains may stay open for over 100 years, providing that when problems do arise they are dealt with. Driving heavy tractors (the big contracting ones) over fields soon disrupts the old clay land drains. Boggy patches in the middle of land that wasn't previously there is more than likely the result of a blockage in a field drain and it can be sorted out with a spade. Water that is seeping out of sloping ground needs channeling into a ditch or cut off drain to save bogging the land below it. If laying a large land drain in a boggy area, a herringbone pattern emptying into a ditch is the normal method employed. Unless the ditches around a field are maintained, the land drains will have little to empty into and may burst back into a low area of ground adjacent to the ditch. Everything must have a gentle fall even if it's only 1:1000. Once a new land drain has been instigated, or an old one repaired, it will only be a matter of days before the land becomes significantly drier.

If you are considering some short runs of DIY drainage work, be advised that the drainage trench needs to be at least 60cm (2ft) deep. The trench need only be dug a spade's width or with a narrow trenching bucket. Unroll your pipe into the trench (any slotted pipe will do) and shovel in stone until the pipe is just covered. If you are laying a herringbone pattern or running one drain into another, throw in a load of rocks or large stones at the junction, this will serve to keep the earth from closing off the drain. Backfill your trench with the spoil to finish; inevitably there will be more spoil than trench space. A roller is handy to help compact the soil a little.

A Temporary Pond

When we first acquired a flock of geese I thought it would be rather nice if they had a little bit of a pond. As a temporary measure, and to avoid time spent digging, I dreamt up a novel way of creating a temporary pool to keep the hissing gaggle quiet. A simple pond can be made from a ton bulk bag of the type used to deliver gravel or sand. Simply fold over all the sides so that the bag becomes half its depth. Line the now fairly rigid bag with a piece of polythene and the pond will hold a significant amount of water. Judicious use of some large rocks in the pool will help stop the edges of the bag becoming downtrodden and give something for the geese to exit the pond from. A ramp of some description will allow the birds into the water.

Hey, it's not rocket science but it was made from what was lying around, solved a problem and it cost nothing. The geese were happy as well.

Build It!

A 10kW wind turbine mounted high up a mast. When rotor speed gets too high, the tail acts to turn the turbine out of the wind.

Chapter Eight
Renewable Energy Projects

We live in a world that statistics show is warming up. Whilst the net causes of global warming are a hotly contested subject, you can be sure that our dependence on crude oil as a power source needs to be diminished. Renewable energy installations on a single property basis are possible to install but in the long term financial rewards are certainly not guaranteed. Government subsidies have done little to allay renewable energy project installation costs; what you gain from grants is soon taken up in costly approved installer schemes. If you want affordable renewable power then you need to to source and fit the equipment yourself and, where necessary, find an electrician to do the crucial parts. Whilst financially speaking the rewards of some areas of renewable energy leave a lot to be desired, you can at least be smug in the knowledge that you're generating it yourself and it's relatively clean.

Simple Solar Water Heater

There's little to add to solar water heating that's not already been said. It's been around for a very long time. I can even remember a guy who had it in the 1980s, yet still it is not used widely enough. Broadly speaking, there are two types of solar collectors known as flat plate and evacuated tube. The flat plate collectors are easy to make and will do a tip top job of heating water during the warmer months. The evacuated tube collectors, whilst not cheap, are able to make use of solar energy all year round, even in northern latitudes. Whereas a flat plate collector will make hot water on a warm day, a tube collector will heat water to a higher than ambient temperature even on an overcast day, thus reducing the further heat input needed. If you want to investigate installing a solar water heating system further,

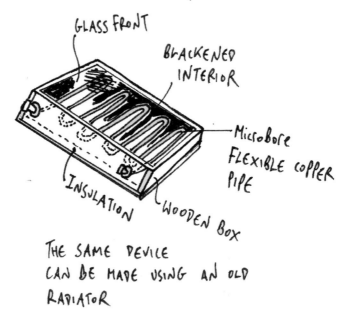

SIMPLE SOLAR WATER HEATER

GLASS FRONT

BLACKENED INTERIOR

MicroBore FLEXIBLE COPPER PIPE

INSULATION

WOODEN BOX

THE SAME DEVICE CAN BE MADE USING AN OLD RADIATOR

METHODS OF PLUMBING

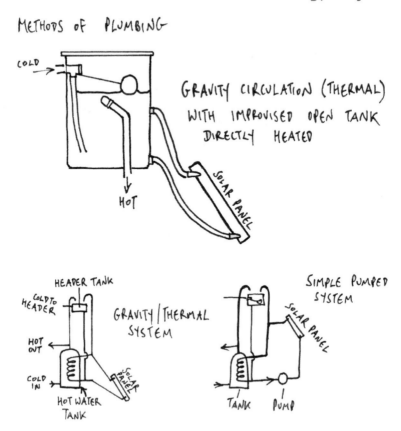

GRAVITY CIRCULATION (THERMAL)
WITH IMPROVISED OPEN TANK
DIRECTLY HEATED

COLD

HOT

SOLAR PANEL

HEADER TANK

COLD TO HEADER

GRAVITY/THERMAL SYSTEM

SIMPLE PUMPED SYSTEM

HOT OUT

COLD IN

SOLAR PANEL

HOT WATER TANK

TANK   PUMP

SOLAR PANEL

CAT (the Centre for Alternative Technology) produce a pamphlet entitled "Tapping the Sun – a guide to solar water heating." There are also some fairly good deals being offered on the internet. Check out www.navitron.org.uk for budget renewable gear. It's also worth scouring eBay for any other deals.

You can, in the meantime, have a bit of fun experimenting with solar water heating. It's very easy to make a flat plate collector and here are a few plans and ideas to get you started. At the simplest level, an old steel radiator painted black will form the basis of a solar water heater, obviously the bigger the better. A step on from this would be to build a box around the radiator, add some insulation at the sides and rear and put a sheet of double glazing 6 inches in front of it. If you don't have an old radiator to hand then the conventional method of making a collector is with loops of pipe laid out in an insulated box behind glass. Microbore (10mm) copper pipe is about £30 for 25 metres and is ideal for this sort of task. I've no experience of using plastic pipe for making a collector. It may work but bear in mind that modern 15mm barrier pipes are not rated for boiling liquids and on a hot day it would be feasible to get close to this in the collector. If the collector is set up on a lower level than the hot water tank, the system will thermo siphon and the water will circulate with the warm water rising to the highest point in the system. If you do not situate your collector lower than the storage tank, you will need a pumped system.

Installing a Ground Source Heat Pump

The ground on which we live acts as a great big heat sink for the sun's energy. During the summer, the earth in the UK warms up and during the winter it cools down. Dig down about 6ft and you will find that the temperature is isothermal; that is to say it stays about the same all year round. Ground source heat pumps make use of this extensive low grade heat and turn it into something usable. In my area this ground temperature is about 4°c.

The advantage of a heat pump is that you get up to 4 times the amount of energy out than you put in. I have a 1kW rated pump and I get 4kW of heat out of it. For those of you who aren't scientists, it works something like this:

The heat pump contains a liquid refrigerant which, when warmed slightly, will evaporate. Basic physics tells us that if you compress a gas you will get heat out of it. In the case of our gaseous refrigerant, the compressor will also return the refrigerant back to its liquid state.

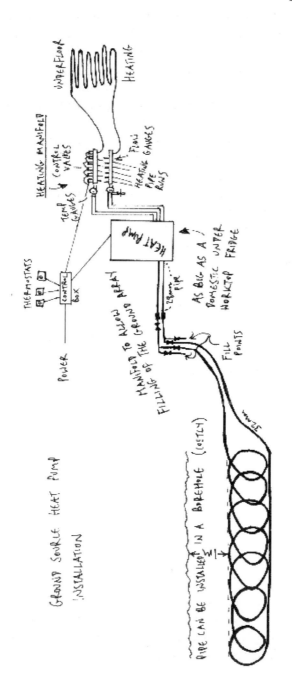

GROUND SOURCE HEAT PUMP INSTALLATION

Build It!

The internal workings of a ground source heat pump.

The refrigerant cycle is closed. There are 2 points where heat is transferred via conductive heat exchangers. Heat is moved from the ground array to the refrigerant closed loop and from the refrigerant loop to the heating system. As the refrigerant is compressed back to its liquid state, heat generated by the gas compression is transferred to the heating output.

Liquid at about zero degrees is pumped from the heat pump out into the ground array where it warms up by 3 or 4°C as it passes through the pipework. This small temperature rise is enough to evaporate the refrigerant in the heat pump back to the start of the cycle.

The heat output is between 35 and 40°C to the heating system. It is possible to increase this figure but the overall efficiency of the system will drop significantly. By trying to work the unit in overdrive to gain higher output temperatures, a point is reached where you are gaining little and an immersion heater would be just as effective.

The companies supplying heat pumps and underfloor heating systems appear to use a one size fits all generic computer program to determine what size pump will suit your house. I won't bore you with the list of engineering qualifications held between a close neighbour and myself but I can categorically say that the simple 'slot your details

Underfloor heating manifold indicating output and return temperatures and loop flow rates.

into our computer program approach' is flawed in many circumstances. The only way to determine what size pump you need is to undertake scientific heat loss calculations for your property.

As the output of a ground source heat pump is termed low grade heat, the house needs to be well insulated to make use of it. Roof insulation is not enough. The walls will need at least 50mm of polystyrene or 25mm of Kingspan or Celotex. Current building regulations require 50mm of foil backed insulation which would certainly make more effective use of a heat pump. Because the heat is low grade, in order to dissipate it there needs to be ample surface area of heating pipework; oversize radiators or wet underfloor heating are the options, the latter beating the former hands down. Unfortunately there is little correlation or cooperation between the suppliers of ground source heat pumps and underfloor heating systems. This means that you are left with an educated gamble as to how much pipework you will need for your property. For heat pump systems, the underfloor pipework needs to be laid at between 100 and 150mm spacing between pipes. Each outlet on the system manifold will supply heating to about 100m of pipework. If you exceed 100m per manifold feed, you will essentially end up with sections of pipe with cool water running through them. My humble abode has about 70m² of floorspace and I am running in the order of 450 metres of underfloor heating through a 6 port manifold.

The advantage of sourcing a UK manufactured heat pump is that you will get customer service and technical support and you may even qualify for a government grant. Kensa Engineering were my chosen suppliers and they were very helpful. As the designated sub-contractor, I did all the work and they offered technical commissioning support. After a £1200 grant, the unit cost an additional £2000. Having spent around £800 on heating components and £150 on a 3 ton excavator, I reckon to have spent £3k. Although imported heat pumps are available for about £1000 direct from China I'm not convinced, as there's no service or guarantees with these machines.

Installation

The 300m of 32mm plastic pipe (slinky) are buried underground in 1m diameter coils. The trench required for this job had a metre deep 30 yard lead trench to a 30 metre long trench of 2 metres depth. All pipework and coils are therefore buried to at least 1 metre in depth. Trench backfill was with the excavated spoil minus any large rocks. A word of advice: a 1.5 ton mini-digger will struggle to dig at 2m depth and may lack the reach so hire a 2.5 – 3 ton machine. Plumbing between the slinky and the heat pump is via an outdoor filling manifold. Once connected to the heat pump with 28mm speedfit plumbing, the slinky has to be filled with antifreeze and purged of air. To do this a powerful electric pump is needed. Antifreeze is circulated out of a dustbin or other suitable container and through the pipework back into the bin until all the airlocks are removed.

I'm not sure that household underfloor heating can be retrofitted without a lot of heartache. Basically, all the downstairs ceilings would have to come down so that pipes can be fixed to the underside of the floors above. Insulation is nailed up underneath the installed heating pipes in order to deflect warmth upward. I fitted my ground floor with underfloor heating by laying a new floor on a 3x2″ timber framework. The 3″ gap allowed for more insulation under the pipework and a concrete biscuit mix around the pipes to aid thermal conductivity. The final flooring job was boarded and tiled and has raised the overall level by about four inches. It does work though.

From a technical point of view there is one electrical connection that has to be made which could require an electrician. Point aside, this type of project is simply a grand wet plumbing job and does not at the time of writing require CORGI or some other quango to preside over it. No doubt in time things will change but at present installation costs can still be kept to a minimum, making this idea a practical alternative to a costly installed central heating system.

Wind Power

Official statistics (which can be found with a quick internet search) show that in this green and pleasant land the wind apparently blows for about 20% of the time overland to about 30% off shore. This admittedly does vary from place to place but you sure as hell are not going to find loads more wind than 30%. Unfortunately, these figures barely make the 'plug and play' 1kW wind turbines on offer from several companies a sensible investment on purely financial grounds. If we take 25% wind as a happy medium, then we can work out for a 1kW turbine that 24 hours x 365 days x 0.25(wind factor) x 1(turbine rating kWh) = 2190 kWh per year.

Build It!

Small 400kW wind turbine. This device is mounted far too close to the building and will be adversely affected by turbulence.

If electricity costs 10p per kWh then the device has potentially saved us a theoretical maximum of £219 a year. Now that appears all well and good but it is theoretical and does not take into account several factors. Firstly the calculation only holds for a system that can make use of all the produced energy 24/7 and does not account for electrical and inverter losses. Battery banks or net metering (selling back to the grid) systems do make use of all the available energy output; household grid tie inverters do not. If you just have a grid tie inverter, your excess power is simply diverted through a "dump load" outlet. This can be somewhat alleviated by dumping energy into domestic hot water tanks.

Poor positioning is the greatest cause of system inefficiency. What the manufacturers tell you little about is the difference between laminar and turbulent airflow on a turbine. Very few small units are likely to be situated in ideal situations where the oncoming airflow is laminar and thus the turbine is working at optimum efficiency. Buildings, trees and topography are all contributing factors in local airflow conditions. If your turbine is not 6 metres up a pole in an uninterrupted airflow, then the likelihood is it may not be working efficiently.

On a recent site visit to a 10kW plant the statistics showed that the real power generation figure was not in the order of 25% but worked out at about 17.5% of the turbine's rating across the year. The payback time for this unit inevitably was in the order of 19 years. The turbine was in an ideal position up a 60 plus foot mast and the electricity was being fed straight into the grid; this was a thorough professionally planned and installed job. Don't over estimate your own site potential. If calculating system payback time, it is wise to note that many systems have not been manufactured and proven long enough to determine whether the unit life will equate to the overall system payback time. The unit could be knackered or outdated before you break even.

Let's put it simply; electricity is still too cheap to force any impetus towards mass take up on micro wind projects. The wind doesn't blow 24 hours a day and when it does blow it may produce more than you can use. Don't get me wrong, they have their place but the installation costs have to be kept low to ever reap any financial benefit. In a town you would be likely to save more on your electricity bill by switching off all of those 'on standby' power parasites than by switching to a trendy windmill.

Years ago I built a reasonably powerful working wind turbine which sadly sat and rusted on my parents back yard until it was scrapped. It took a lot of time and cost quite a bit. With what's now available for £350 or less, it would barely seem worth the trouble today

If designing your own system or if you have the intention of buying one, there are some serious questions that need to be answered:

What do you want to do with the power? a. Sell it to the grid,

Build It!

b. Feed it straight into the household mains or c. Charge a battery bank.

How much power do you need?

a. From Question 1a. What's the maximum the National grid will allow you to feed in locally? (often less than 10kWh).

b. If feeding power directly into the mains, the ability to provide a background level of power via a grid tie inverter may be all you are wanting.

c. If charging batteries to fulfill all your energy needs you could get a changeover switch fitted to your mains supply and run your house from the batteries with a large inverter. If your power system runs low, switch back over to mains.

d. Consider system architecture. Some turbines will keep generating at low wind speed but are limited at the top end, others vice versa.

Is your site suitable for the system you have in mind (consider turbulence, maximum wind conditions, the civil engineering aspect, visual amenity and planning restrictions).

As regards cost, some may feel that the environmental benefits outweigh the cost. There's a balance in everything.

If a turbine is to be positioned a long way from the house or battery bank, you will need to consider power losses in the cable. As a general rule, keep losses to a minimum by transmitting voltages as high as possible (thereby minimising current levels which exacerbate power loss). 36 volts is better than 24v is better than 12v (is better than none!).
China has a long pedigree in wind turbine manufacture as large tracts of the country are off grid. The downside to imported products is the availability of spares and support if they do go wrong. There are some tidy UK models available

for between £500 - 700, although don't forget this is without inverters and in many cases rigging and poles. Buy the best quality you can afford. If it's possible that you can view one of your proposed machines in action it will be worth it and an obvious opportunity to resolve any operational or technical queries you may have before purchasing.

Photovoltaic (PV) Solar Panels

PV panels generate electricity out of sunlight, a minor miracle perhaps. For those seriously interested in renewable power there is good news. In the past few years the cost of electricity producing solar panels has dropped like a stone. Panels rated at 180watts can now be had for a shade under £500 each. If you do the maths, you will find that with some careful planning, three or four of these units will produce sufficient power to run an average household. You will, however, need an energy storage system or the facility to sell back to the grid. The beauty of solar is that it is predictable and you can work out reliable estimates of a system's potential before you start. Obviously, you will need sufficient space to mount the panels but at least they don't appear as intrusive to onlookers as a wind turbine and neither do they hum and sing when working hard. Panels need careful alignment towards the sun. Tracking mounts can be purchased which, although expensive, track the sun and thus align the panel to get the best electrical output. Panels don't have to be mounted on a roof. A south facing ground installation will work just as well if you have enough unshaded space.

If using PV panels to charge a battery, a charge controller is needed. This has two effects. Firstly it prevents overcharging and damage to the batteries and secondly it contains diodes (electrical one way valves) which prevent the panels from going into a reverse mode where they use energy from the batteries at night.

Build It!

Hydro electric scheme at Bonfield Ghyll, North Yorkshire Moors, photographs courtesy of the National Trust.

Micro Hydro Systems

By which we mean a broad brush of water driven power sources. Water has been used for hundreds of years if not more to drive crude mills and suchlike. Large scale water power got its first real airing courtesy of Richard Arkwright who was arguably one of the kick starters of the industrial revolution with his water powered cotton mills. Water is the most productive of all renewable energy sources and if you have a suitable stream or river on your property that you have not exploited you should get cracking right away. As long as you are able to obtain a fall of at least 3ft and have sufficient volume of water running along your watercourse, then power generation could be for you. As rivers generally flow 24 hours a day (droughts aside) micro hydro is probably the best renewable source there is. To my knowledge there are few companies in the UK manufacturing small hydro electric plants so most of what is available is either bespoke, manufactured or imported. Take a look at www.navitron.org.uk for information on such units. You will be surprised at how little they actually cost.

There are turbines available to suit both low and high head applications. On a National Trust farm in the North

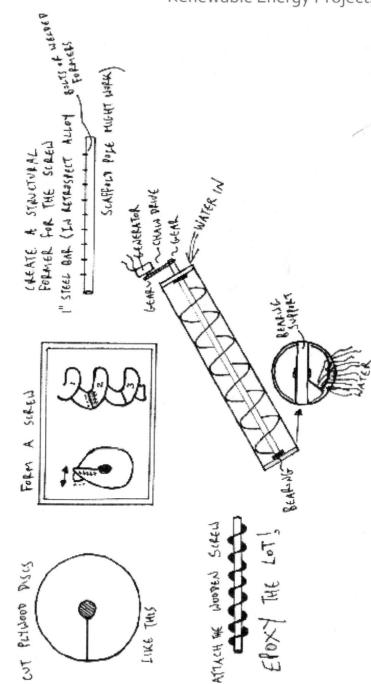

Build It!

Yorkshire Moors they are using a large Archimedes screw coupled to a generator in order to successfully generate power for a remote sheep farm. The fall of water in this instance is in the order of seven or eight feet and the unit should operate down to flow levels as little as 20 litres per second. Various examples of these devices can be seen in action at www.howshamhydro.co.uk. The machines, I believe, are of German design and manufacture and, whilst impressive, look typically over engineered with plenty of redundant capacity.

Having pondered the difficulty in building a similar screw that will work for small stream applications, I made a paper model and am convinced that it could be done on a DIY basis. The difficulty is in producing a straight screw that will rotate in a true fashion; steel would present considerable engineering difficulties with limited tooling. I am interested in creating a screw prototype manufactured in laminated epoxy over a wooden screw former attached to a steel shaft. A test unit of approximately 10ft in length and 1ft in diameter would theoretically provide a useful power output if geared and connected to a small dynamo. Bear in mind that these units operate slowly, somewhere in the order of 40 - 60rpm.

Before buying or fabricating a hydro electric system, you need to first asses the power that your stream can provide. Remember from school physics that Potential Energy = mgh where m = mass, g = acceleration due to gravity (9.81) and h = height. Energy is measured in joules, but technically a watt of electrical power is a joule per second.

Assessing the flow of your stream may prove more difficult. If it's a small stream, you could divert it through a gap and see how long it takes to fill a bucket. The other option is to work out the average cross sectional area and then observe and measure the flow rate between points. If the cross section of water were $0.7 \times 0.3 = 0.21$ m² and the flow were measured as 0.75m/s, then the flow rate would be 0.1575 m³/s or 157 litres a second. If we were to send this flow over a 2m drop then the total theoretical potential energy would work out at approximately 3000 joules per second. If it were possible to covert all this energy to electricity (it isn't), it would equate to 3kWh.

The central bar on which a screw generator could be formed would need to be straight in the first place and either 25mm or 38mm thick. The screw formers are to be made from 4mm ply and are simply cut as 300mm discs with a corresponding 25 or 38mm hole in the centre. A straight perpendicular cut is made between the centre hole and the outside edge of each disc. By taking a number of these discs (try it with paper first) it is possible to join them together so that the edge of the slot in one is fixed to the edge of the slot the next disc. Keep doing this and all the discs will be joined together in a stack; pull the top and bottom discs apart and you will get a big wooden spiral. In the first instance, the joins should be made with copper wire or fine cable ties. These joints are then carefully taped and epoxied. This is not madness. I do have a Marine Technology degree in ship engineering and other such matters. These plywood and epoxy techniques are known as stitch and tape and are used to build large and small boats alike.

The steel bar will need marking, holes drilling and spacer pins placing to which the screw can fit against, prior to laminating. These pins would perhaps require a tack weld to hold them in place. I haven't got as far as designing bearing blocks but commercially available sealed units could be used, set into a substantial cross member top and bottom. I'd consider having the steel bar and its pins either galvanised or powder coated prior to starting the screw thread. Set the pitch of the screw at about 13 degrees to the horizontal. The wooden ply spring can be mounted onto the steel bar. Tightening it slightly at one end will help shape the thread. To achieve a good job with epoxy resin and glass or carbon fibre takes patience. It also helps if you've done a bit of practicing beforehand. I spent years fibre glassing a leaky yacht that subsequently became named Sea Bitch and still couldn't get it right (think that's funny? the tender was known as Son of a ....). A large supply of disposable gloves are essential. By my estimation, the screw would require at least 3 good tidy laminations on each side. That's as far as I've got. The screw has to fit into a length of pipe or a concrete half pipe casting. I'd suggest finding the pipe first and building the screw to fit. I'm also persuaded that the gears and chain off a bike might come in handy as a cheap gearbox. Bear in mind that this machine would work if made with a bit of TLC. It would also be inexpensive, probably a few hundred quid as opposed to the very nice but costly Teutonic engineering I've seen.

Integrated Power Systems

The real answer to micro generation projects lies in a holistic approach. Integrated micro generation should not focus on one particular aspect of renewable energy but use the sum of two or more inputs to achieve the overall requirements. The use of wind, solar PV and water heating as individual elements can contribute a little to personal energy requirements but considered as a whole, it is likely that between 60 and 75% of overall household energy requirements would be met. Quantifying the previous statement, we are not regarding large installations but rather projects that might comprise a solar water heater, 2 high power PV panels and a wind turbine rated between 500w to 1kW. On a DIY basis such an installation might be achieved for as little as £3500 based on current researched prices. Depending on location, power storage and management facilities it is feasible that 100% of personal energy requirements could be met in this way. It is an outrage that with on the shelf technology available there is little commercial drive to produce housing with such features installed as normal spec.

Renewable Source Lighting

Whilst you may not have the capacity to generate all your energy requirements, it would be a great achievement if as many people as possible could power just their lighting from renewable means. At the time of writing this I have the following lights switched on in the house:

3 energy savers @ 9w
7 energy savers @ 11w

As we are in the depths of deepest winter, 5 of these lights are on for about 11 hours and the rest might be on for 9 hours. A bit of maths tells me that $5 \times 11w \times 11hrs = 605$ w/h ; $((3 \times 9) + (2 \times 11)) \times 9hrs = 441w/h$.

At this rate of usage (I am guilty of having unnecessary lights on) I am using $605 + 441/1000 = 1.05$ kWh a day on lighting. Assuming there are 7.5 hours of daylight at the moment, we can work out that a 180w PV panel would generate a theoretical maximum of 1.35 kWh. Truthfully it wouldn't, due to dull days etc. There are also inverter losses to account for. In reality one might get 0.65 kWh of usable, stored power on a winter's day. The point is, 0.65 would drive five 11w energy saving bulbs for nigh on 11 hours a day, losses accounted for. I, and many of you, could tailor my light usage to one 180w solar panel running into 2 deep storage batteries and a low powered inverter. The panel costs £500, a charge controller costs about £50, the batteries are available for £100 and a low power inverter costs about £25. There is probably still change out of a thousand pounds to find some qualified electrical help for the bits you can't manage.

Alternative Fuels and Electric Vehicles (EV's)

I have been in contact with several individuals who have successfully converted existing cars into electric vehicles.

Build It!

Perhaps the most successful one to be found on the internet is at www.solarvan.co.uk. By taking an existing lightweight vehicle design, removing the engine and fitting a motor you could effectively do away with your fuel bills. Sounds simple? Apparently it actually is. Typical conversion times are in the order of two days work with a suitable donor vehicle. Reliant Kittens, small Fiats and mini vans are a few of the preferred candidates. There is no road tax, low insurance is available and if you convert a van there is no MOT required. Before discussing this further let's look at the drawbacks. The range of these vehicles is limited by battery capacity; batteries are often heavy and small cars have a limited carrying capacity. Recent innovations have seen a move away from lead acid batteries to lithium ion cells. Li-ion batteries offer huge advantages to car designers in terms of weight, size and power, but they don't half cost a lot so for the first time EV builder, lead acid is probably going to have to do.

A very light EV running on lead acid with a suitable DC motor would be capable of achieving 50 mph, would cruise at around 40 and would have a range of about 40 miles. The cost of converting a vehicle would be around £1500 according to my sources who have done it. I am told that a Lynch motor is the preferred power plant for lightweight projects and, having studied the designs and information on their website, it is definitely worth a look. The only technical problem that cannot be immediately purchased to build an EV is the mounting plate required to join the motor to the car's transmission. With a little skill, however, you could make one with plate steel, an angle grinder and a drill.

I have researched the use of vegetable oil and bio-diesel as a fuel and have drawn the following conclusions, which I'll share with you. Common rail diesel engines will, in a short time, experience injector trouble unless the manual specifically endorses the use of these fuels. Other standard injection vehicles are OK. It is possible to manufacture bio-diesel from oil but you will require a processing plant. The plans to build a plant are available on the internet or else you will have to pay anywhere between £295 and £700 for a small one.

Clean new vegetable oil works well in diesel engines in warm weather. The water content of previously used veg oil is too high and needs reducing, either by evaporation or water absorbing beads or gel. Mixed in proportion with straight road diesel, veg oil will work all year round (don't use more than 60% oil in the winter). A simple pre-heater conversion kit that warms the oil will allow you to run on straight veg oil all year round. I have also read that by mixing 5% petrol into vegetable oil the fuel will work at lower temperatures, unadjusted. I have not tried this but shall give it a short trial. I would suggest that whilst it may work it will increase the cylinder head temperature of the engine and may affect carbonation. It would certainly be best trialled in an older car. Some engines (particularly Mercedes) have been proven to give years of trouble free running on vegetable oil, but others do not like it. It has also been proven that damage to engines occurs on starting and shutting down. Systems that allow switching of fuels once the engine has warmed up are inexpensive to install and can alleviate many potential damage problems.

Possible Methane Digester Plant (not for the faint hearted)

It never ceases to amuse me how scientists are starting to attribute 18% (according to Radio 4) of the world's carbon problems to farming. Perhaps we should ban it and learn to live on fresh air. Talk about trying to sink an industry that already hasn't had the best of recent years. Modernisation is, in part, leading food production up a garden path to greater carbon impact, not less. Grow your own food is my advice. There might come a day when you need it.

Methane Digester

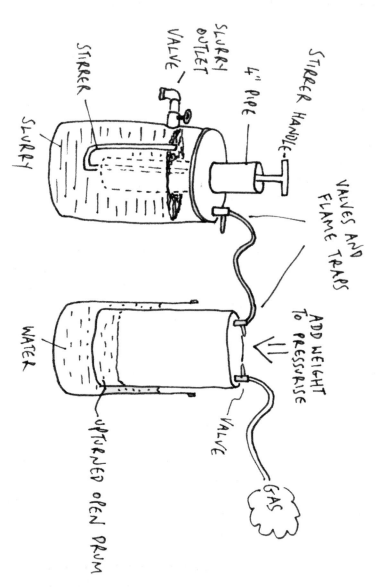

STIRRER HANDLE

SLURRY OUTLET VALVE

4" PIPE

STIRRER

SLURRY

SLURRY

VALVES AND FLAME TRAPS

ADD WEIGHT TO PRESSURISE

WATER

VALVE

UPTURNED OPEN DRUM

GAS

Undoubtedly one of the great wastes of farming is that oft talked about by product, methane. Yes, blame it on the dairy cows, but large herds of wild animals are emitting the same all over Africa. It is surprising that so few production plants exist in the UK that can utilise the gas coming from vast quantities of animal dung and slurry. Building regulations are so fraught with ventilation problems on septic tank

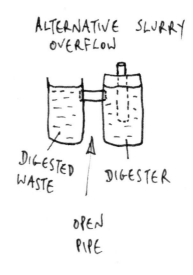

installations that no one seems to have considered altering their design to capture the useful gas segment. Yet among all this, the late John Seymour's epic self -sufficiency book listed a description and image of a methane digester as early as 1976. Although it illustrates the principle beautifully, it is not an obvious guide to manufacture. Methane digesters are not rocket science but they do require very careful planning, construction, siting and operation if mishaps and worse are to be avoided.

The following information is intended as a guide to the workings of one of these plants. It is not conclusive as I have not tried it myself. If one were hypothetically to build such a unit it would have to be trialled at the far end of a field, away from buildings, livestock and other potential hazards. It's an interesting possibility, but for most of you it should remain such. My responsibility ends here.

This plant is my variation on other schemes I have witnessed. It is designed with components that you could easily get hold of, so it is not on a purely conceptual basis.

Firstly, once in operation, methane digesters will, in theory, break down all manner of greenery in much the same way as a mammal's gut. In practice it is difficult to get the digestion process started unless the temperature of the unit is kept at between 20 and 30°C. Gas output is directly in proportion to digester temperature. Once established, the process should deal with a wide array of animal slurries. It should be noted, however, that cow dung is widely regarded as the tool of choice to get the process working.

The unit comprises a digester and a gas storage container. A second storage unit could be added for increased capacity. The digester comprises a large plastic or steel drum. The drum needs to be airtight and to have a means of adding slurry, a means of removing slurry and a means of stirring the mixture in the tank. A piece of 100mm (4″) pipe should be let into the top of the drum, extending down through the tank to about 30cm from the bottom. A bent steel stirring rod could be located in this tube on fitting. It's necessary to achieve a good seal at the union between the drum top and the 4″ pipe as the top of the tank will end up being pressurised with gas. The drum needs a slurry outlet and there are two options. The first is to use a manually operated valve and simply remove the same amount of slurry that you first put in. If you get your slurry levels wrong and they fall to the overflow level, you will lose pressure from this outlet. The second option is an automatic overflow into another open drum. As slop is added through the 4″ pipe, it displaces the topmost overflow into a separate container. Simply remove the amount you just put in from the open container. The whole of the production unit needs to be heavily lagged and insulated.

The gas storage facility is little more than one inverted, cut off drum that simply fits inside another. By adding a level of water between the two, the gas container is sealed. Gas is fed into and out of this device. A degree of pressurisation can be obtained by adding weight to the top of the storage tank. Modern gas cooker connection hoses have flame traps and shut offs built into them and one or more of these should be employed in the lines between the drums, especially on the gas supply out. Additionally, a shut off valve should be located after each stage.

The beauty of this design is that it's simple. More gas tanks could be added, if required. The length of time that the unit takes to digest material varies according to temperature, as do most chemical reactions. Seymour quotes figures ranging from 2 weeks to one month. The implications of this are that the amount of slurry added per day will have to be varied according to circumstance. Various figures bandied about on the internet have daily slurry replacement volumes varying from between 2 and 8%. In the climate of the UK I'd suggest that the off gassing rate would be slow and that 2% of a 200 litre barrel that's about ¾ full would amount to little more than 3 litres of cow dung a day. Once you've managed to get a plant running it'll digest practically any crap you'd care to throw at it. Be advised though, it will need a daily stir and feed, but then again, if you have the animals in the first place, that shouldn't be a problem.

What can the gas be used for? It could be piped away and used to run a heater. I'd be interested to see if it would power a small petrol generator, although the carbon dioxide content may be too high to successfully run a petrol engine.

Build It!

Chest in use. In this version, a removable draw was fitted inside.

Chapter Nine
The 'Odds and Sods' Section

A Double Bed

This project was undertaken some years ago, solely to provide a bed for a little used spare room. We could have bought one but the burst of inspiration to construct a bed came from a trendy book. I sketched out my design on a scrap of paper to get an idea of the quantity of materials required. Reclaimed wood formed the basis of this project and a local reclamation yard provided the necessaries for a meagre seven quid. A power sander was used to renovate all the wood and the various pieces were painted with several coats of a fairly thin flooring varnish which gave the timber a bit of lustre.

The timber used for this project was as follows. Please bear in mind that mattress sizes are still manufactured to imperial

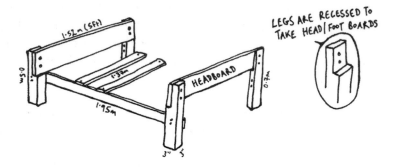

measurements and so is much of the reclaimed timber you will find. Thus a real mix of measurement units ensues:

Legs - 3 x 3″ (76mm²) was used for 2 legs of 0.5m in length and 2 legs of 0.7m in length.
Bed ends – 7 x 1⅜″ (approximately 178 x 35mm).
2 lengths of 1.524m (5ft).
Side planks – 4½ x 1″ (114 x 25mm),
2 lengths of 1.95m.
Base planks – These were old lengths of ¾″ thick floor board.
8 pieces of 1.37m (4′6″) length were used.

The main structure of the bed was bolted using M6 coach bolts with appropriate washers and nuts. 2 bolts were used per joint. The base planks for the mattress to lie on were secured using suitable length screws.

Construction method

All the wood was cut to length and thoroughly sanded prior to assembly. The bed legs all had wood removed (as illustrated) to accommodate both the headboard and foot board. Holes were drilled using a 6mm drill and were 4″ apart. Two legs were bolted to each 5ft headboard and foot board using 2 bolts per side. This produced two separate bed ends that needed to be joined together using the long side planks. The side timbers are now attached to the bed end that will go at the foot end of the bed. The side timbers are mounted on the inside of the bed legs. The side timbers should be marked, drilled and bolted high enough up the inside of the bed leg as to be touching the head/foot board above them.

Always mark the position of any holes prior to drilling. Use a suitably long 6mm drill and drill two holes through each bed leg from the outside. Holes should be central on the leg and positioned one above the other with a 2.5″ vertical spacing.

Once bolted squarely at the foot end of the bed, the side planks can be attached at the headboard end. The side planks should be bolted at an equal height on all four bed legs and the mattress planks spaced equally across the bed frame and screwed down into the side timbers.

Sea Chest/Blanket Box

This project was made by Pat Crawford, a good friend of ours, who favours wood reclaimed from delivery pallets to build his creations. Aside from chicken houses, fencing and the usual run of the mill stuff that can be made from pallet wood, Pat has demonstrated that you can turn fairly rough timber into attractive and usable day to day furniture. When tidying up rough wood, a power plane is desirable. Even better than a power plane is a thicknesser, although you'd be unlikely to find one of these for less than £150. A thicknesser is a fixed, adjustable plane that allows you to feed wood into it. It has automatic feed rollers and it will reduce timber to the required uniform size. It doesn't really matter if the wood is tatty looking as long as it is not rotten. If wood is damp, it really does need to be left under cover for a while in order to dry out. Slightly damp wood doesn't cut, sand or plane well and you will certainly not obtain a decent finish.

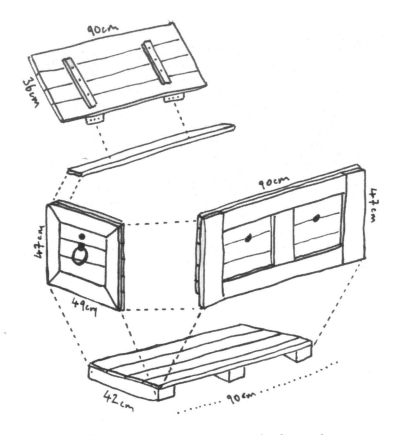

The pallet used in this instance consisted of wooden staves approximately 17mm thick and 190mm in width.

Base – The base measures 90 x 42cm. Planks cut to 90cm in length are simply nailed to three pieces of 42cm long timber (such as 3 x 2″). The sides of the box are made individually before being assembled together. It is easiest to explain this with the diagrams. The small sides measure 49cm long x 47 deep. The long sides 90 x 47cm and the top 90 x 36cm. The sides are fixed to the base and each other with suitable screws and nails. The sides are fastened to the edges of the base and do not sit on top of it. Strap hinges are used to secure the lid to an additional plank fixed to the top of the box. The top edges of the box are finished with a patterned

Note the use of patterned mouldings to cover the corners and edges.

40 x 10mm architrave. By protruding the architrave above the top edge of the box, a recess is formed into which the lid closes. Architraves are also used to cover the joints on all 4 corners.

The box was finished with a dark wood stain and steel ring handles were fitted at each end for carrying. Chains were fitted inside to limit the opening of the lid and Pat also made a lovely wooden clasp and pin for the front, which is a little beyond the purpose of this book.

An inch diameter hole was drilled in each end and two at a regular interval in the front, which added to the general overall effect, but also contributed to the airing of the intended purpose; Mrs Crawford had originally wanted a box for storing linen and blankets.

Pat has since built a number of these boxes in a variety of sizes which currently adorn the homes of friends and family around Cornwall. A very worthy creation, Sir.

Doors

When is a door not a door? When it's ajar...........ha ha! As barn doorways come in a multitude of sizes, many of which are not standard, some idea of how to construct a basic plank door or stable door is useful. For a lightweight or internal door, 19mm (¾˝) tongue and groove will suffice. I have tried making a stable door out of this timber and it is not really up to the job. For a heavier door, planks of 25mm (1˝) are necessary. For the bracing to which the door planks are attached, use slightly heavier timber than for the tongue and groove. 150 x 25mm (6 x 1˝) would be fine for a heavy door. Hinge straps need to be fixed with heavy gauge screws or bolts. Doors are best made with oval nails as they can be hammered into the wood and the heads can be lost and filled if necessary. For the Z bracing on the back of the door see the section on making gates; the principle is the same. If making a

A stable door. Note the bracing method and the top lip on the lower door. Old strap hinges are reused.

stable door, make up a Z on the lower door. When you fix the uppermost cross member of the Z, let it protrude 2 inches higher than the level of the door planks. By leaving this lip, it gives something for the upper stable door to close against and it also reduces the draught.

A top stable door will have the two horizontal cross members fairly close together. In this situation, use two diagonal braces eg. //, instead of one.

Roofing Ladder

Smallholdings and farms inevitably have plenty of roof repairs that need doing and a manufactured roofing ladder costs a lot of money. There is, however, a simple kit available that allows for the user to manufacture their own ladder out of 50 x 25mm (2 x 1˝) roofing laths. The kit simply provides the metal hooks to go over the ridge of your roof and a set of small wheels to aid positioning the ladder up and across the tiles.

A roofing ladder made from wooden laths and a ridge hook kit.

The ladder ridge hook from Screwfix costs £26.49 (at the time of print) and can easily be fitted to any ladder. When first put together, I made a ladder that was approximately 4 metres long and with 50cm long rungs spaced every 30cm up the ladder. Ensure that the timber you use doesn't contain any large knots that might break, and use M6 coach bolts, washers and nuts to fasten the rungs to the ladder sides. There are other ways of making ridge hooks but as it's a long way to the ground, 26 quid isn't much and as many of you will not have metalworking facilities, I shan't endeavor to go further.

Raised Beds

The Victorians did a great deal of gardening in raised beds. Apparently they were able to cultivate higher growing temperatures all year round, hence increasing productivity. For me, raised beds have three purposes. Firstly, they are a great way of getting rid of excess soil and spoil from building and gardening projects. Secondly, they can be used to tidy up unsightly or unusable garden areas. Lastly, they can be used as a form of terracing to create a useful growing bed at the bottom of a steep slope.

To form a raised bed, a retaining wall can be built on a permanent or temporary basis. A permanent structure will require cement in its construction and should be built to withstand the weight of soil behind it. Dry stone walling is another way of creating a raised bed that can later be moved, if necessary. The construction technique that I favour is using wooden posts and planks and then backfilling the created space behind them. Build the bed so that it contains sufficient depth of usable soil, remembering that some plants will require more root depth than others. I have made my beds to be about 0.5m deep. Start by knocking in a row of fence posts in a straight line. Position the posts every metre and use a plumb line or a piece of rope to ensure they're in the correct place.

The posts need to be driven in well in order to withstand the soil pressure on the walls of the bed; the posts can be cut to height later on if required. The planks go on the inside of the posts i.e. the posts end up visible on the outside of the bed.

Use planks that are as thick as possible; 50mm will last a lot longer than 25mm. I've used inch thick timber and it seems to last OK for a few years but it will definitely need replacing sooner rather than later. Having listened to Gardeners Question Time on Radio 4, they do not recommend using treated railway sleepers as they apparently go on leaching tar for a long time. Sawmill wood is a good investment for this job and if you want the bed to last a bit longer you could try lining the woodwork with some sort of plastic membrane to stop the damp getting to it. As stated previously, treating timber will increase its life. Use four inch nails to fasten the planks to the stakes. It takes a while to fill a bed up with earth so either build the bed around some pre-positioned piles of loose earth or leave a side off the bed so that you can run in with your wheelbarrow.

I have previously added some old window frames to the top of a raised bed under which we then grew strawberries; at least it stopped the chickens from eating them. If you want to do likewise, nail a piece of timber along the back of your bed that is sturdy enough and positioned in the correct place so that hinges can be screwed into it. This will support your windows or clear plastic top. The only problem with enclosed raised beds and cold frames is that you must remember to water the plants in them regularly.

Dog Kennel

A few years back, our dog arrived courtesy of the next door neighbour's sheepdog and a local collie bitch (no diagrams needed). As chances of cute puppies are a flash in the pan sort of event, they inevitably catch one unprepared. Shortly after taking charge of the pup, I thought that a kennel next to the house would be more ideal than chewed up furniture. The kennel was designed to be made from timber mill offcuts as this was my nearest supply. If using rough sawn wood, you do really need an array of power tools including a bench

Build It!

DOG KENNEL

FLOOR AND UNATTACHED SIDE

saw to regulate the dimensions of the timber.

SIDE PANEL

FLOOR — **NAIL HERE**

VIEW FROM AN END

The kennel is a metre long by 0.6m wide. The floor is made from planks of sawn wood which sit on three 0.6m long blocks. The wooden blocks keep the floor off the ground and can be made from anything between 2 and 3 inches square. The sides are 0.6m high and the roof apex is 0.85m high measured from the floor.

Make up two sides using planks. A 0.5m length of 75 x 38mm (3 x 1½") or similar is screwed in place at each end of the panel. The length of batten should be positioned so that it sits on the baseboard, but the side panel protrudes past the baseboard to floor level. Hopefully the diagrams illustrate this. The side panels can be nailed into the 3 timbers that are supporting the kennel floorboards. If you are making this kennel out of planks as I did, you will need to add a triangle of battening at each end to support the roof. Join the two sides by nailing one 0.6m strip across each end. This will

HORIZONTAL BRACING AT BOTH ENDS

NAILED   NAILED

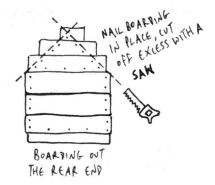

NAIL BOARDING IN PLACE, CUT OFF EXCESS WITH A SAW

BOARDING OUT THE REAR END

help brace the two sides and give supports to attach further timber to. Above these crosspieces you need to form a triangle of wood to support the roof and the ends. Cut two lengths of lath to 40cm and mitre the ends so that the pieces will fit together to form a triangle above the cross member that is bracing the kennel sides.

BOARDING THE FRONT END

The entrance is formed using planks in a vertical, rather than a horizontal plane. Use a plank between 10 and 15cm wide at each side to close the doorway down a little. Fill in the top triangle with vertical boarding. If you wish to have a smaller doorway, simply bring the cladding down a little lower. Use a horizontal piece of plank at the bottom edge of the doorway.

The roof can be made up of scrappy wood but may need an internal length of batten to bring the apex together. Finish the roofing job with a covering of felt that slightly overlaps the kennel sides. Finally, treat the kennel with a proprietary wood treatment product.

Build It!

Further Reading

I have an extensive collection of smallholding and old farming books. These are a few of the titles I have found helpful:

Hooper, T. Guide to Bees & Honey.
Jackson, Day. Complete DIY manual, Collins. (A must for the practically challenged).
Seymour, J. The Complete book of Self Sufficiency, DK. (The best smallholding book by far).
Seymour, J. The Lore of the Land, (Out of Print)   (Perhaps the number onc book on general land management out there).
Thear, Fraser The Complete Book of Raising Livestock and Poultry, PAN.

Listed Suppliers

Navitron - Suppliers of renewable energy equipment
www.navitron.org.uk or www.c-zero.co.uk

Screwfix - catalogue and store based hardware firm
www.screwfix.com

Howarth Timber. My local preferred timber merchant, but they have branches UK wide.

LBS - horticultural products supplier
www.lbsgardenwarehouse.co.uk

Maplin - electronics and electrical components.
www.maplin.co.uk

Thornes - Beekeeping equipment
www.thorne.co.uk

The Good Life Press Ltd
P O Box 536
Preston
PR2 9ZY

01772 652693

We publish a wide range of titles for the smallholder, farmer and country dweller as well as the monthly magazine, Home Farmer.

Other Titles of interest:

A Guide to Traditional Pig Keeping by Carol Harris
An Introduction to Keeping Cattle by Peter King (2008)
An Introduction to Keeping Sheep by J Upton/D Soden
Cider Making by Andrew Lea (2008)
Flowerpot Farming by Jayne Neville (2008)
Grow and Cook by Brian Tucker (2008)
How to Butcher Livestock and Game by Paul Peacock
Making Jams and Preserves by Diana Sutton (2008)
Precycle! by Paul Peacock (2008)
Showing Sheep by Sue Kendrick (2008)
Talking Sheepdogs by Derek Scrimgeour
The Bread and Butter Book by Diana Sutton (2008)
The Cheese Making Book By Paul Peacock
The Polytunnel Companion by Jayne Neville
The Sausage Book by Paul Peacock
The Smoking and Curing Book by Paul Peacock
The Urban Farmer's Handbook by Paul Peacock (2008)

'Build It 2!' by Joe Jacobs will be published in 2009

www.goodlifepress.co.uk
www.homefarmer.co.uk